REMEMBER MY NAME

JENNIFER PULLING

Published by Bealey Publishing
© Copyright 2023 Jennifer Pulling

The right of Jennifer Pulling to be identified as author of
the work has been asserted by her in accordance with
sections 77 and 78 of the Copyrights, Designs and
Patents Act 1988.

ISBN 978-1-8383667-2-8

A CIP catalogue copy for this book is available
from The British Library

Printed on FSC certified paper

DEDICATION

For Andrew, who has shared so many
adventures on our travels together.

Jennifer Pulling

I

They met when their fingers touched. He seized the half empty bottle of wine as she reached towards it. She'd had to burrow through the throng around the heavily laden food table to find it, the only white wine among an assortment of red.

It was 'Matt Damon' she realised, frowning at him. She had dubbed him that on her first glimpse earlier that day. She had been helping Matilde and Salvatore unload an astonishing feast from the car. It was *Pasquetta*, the day after Easter Sunday and a bank holiday in Rome, when so many left the city for a picnic in the country. The man was standing by his car, a low-slung Spyder convertible. Glancing up he caught her eye and smiled. She noted how carelessly he was dressed. Unusual, she thought, for an Italian. Later she walked past him as he stood chatting to the Nanninis, and she saw that he was tall and broad shouldered and his hair was slightly receding.

Now she turned away, from the table with the wine, pushing through the crowd and making for Matilde and her family sitting on the grass.

'Excuse me,' he arrived beside her. Forced to pause she glared at him.

'You wanted this?' He held up the bottle.

'I just don't like red wine,' she said.

'I see, then take it, please.'

She wanted to cut him short. 'It doesn't matter.'

'Is this your first *Pasquetta*?' he persisted. 'I take it you are a tourist. I always say I won't come to these *festicciole* and then end up enjoying them.'

She clicked her tongue and shook her head. 'I'm *not* a tourist, I live in Rome.'

'Ah.' He was eyeing the label on the bottle. 'This isn't very good. You probably wouldn't like it.'

'Maybe not,' she said, amused now by his attempt to delay her.

She felt his gaze travel over her from the stylish cut of her dark hair to her low-cut flowery dress, it was that Italian way of looking she had now grown accustomed to. He held out his hand.

'Giorgio,' he said. 'Giorgio Bevacqua.'

'Amy Armstrong.'

'Well Amy, shall we see if there is a secret store of white wine somewhere?'

She glanced back at the groups of people who had become her friends during the past, eventful year. No one seemed to be looking for her. She felt a twinge of guilt for the absent Davide. But it's only a drink, she told herself.

'Come on then,' He led the way to another part of the field and she saw there was indeed another table, this one loaded with bottles.

'Now let me see.' He picked up one bottle, considered the label, then another as if they were expensive wines, which she was sure they were not.

'I think this one you'll like.'

As she watched him fill two glasses she felt a sudden sense of gratitude that she, Amy Armstrong, was here, now, on this April day 1998. The sun was warm on her bare arms and the city she had made her adopted home a few miles away.

'You look happy,' Giorgio's voice came to her.

'I am. Who wouldn't be, here?'

'Good,' he said. They clinked glasses. 'May all your wishes come true.'

They drank in a companionable silence.

He held up the bottle. 'Another?'

But an image of Davide came to her mind, he seated across the table from her at *Grappolo d'Oro* on the evening of their first dinner together. It was the night he'd admitted he came to the cat sanctuary not to adopt a cat but to find her, the night he had kissed her for the first time.

'I should get back to my friends. They might be looking for me.' But she hesitated, meeting Giorgio's gaze. 'Or perhaps they could wait a little longer.'

He smiled 'I'm sure they'd understand.'

Understand what? She asked herself. This man means nothing to me. But as they finished the bottle between them and then sought shade under an oak tree to laugh

7

and talk, she thought why not? It is just an enjoyable afternoon interlude with someone I'll never see again.

He asked her about her life in Rome and she told him about her spice stall in Campo de Fiori. He listened attentively. He was clearly impressed by her success and expressed admiration of the way she had built her clientele.

'Yes, I had my doubts whether I'd succeed here and people were a bit reluctant to try at first.'

'Interesting when you remember the ancient Romans used a lot of spices, herbs too. Cumin, for example, it was widely used in ancient Rome, ground to a paste and spread on bread. Pliny never tired of it.'

She did not say she knew this already, having made a study for the presentations she gave from time to time.

'Wasn't fennel one of their favourites?' She asked.

'Yes, they used it medicinally too. It was believed to give courage and strength.' He caught her questioning glance. 'How do I know all this? I'm an archaeologist, you see. I particularly enjoy studying the domestic life of these bygone people on our digs.'

It was her turn to have her interest piqued.

'The Etruscans,' he replied in answer to her question, 'such a mysterious civilisation.'

Amy realised they had been sitting there for over two hours and had not stopped talking. Giorgio had a delightfully relaxed manner that was so different from the often-nervous Davide. He laughed easily and gave her his full attention when she told him about her work at Largo Argentina with the cats.

'Some of them have been abandoned and others are brought in off the streets. There was one we called Mister Grumpy who became such a sweet natured creature. All they ask for is some love.'

'I'd never have put you down as a crazy cat lady.'

Her tone was cool at his use of 'crazy.' 'Appearances can be very deceptive!'

'Oops! Sorry!'

For the first time in months she was enjoying another man's company. And why shouldn't I? She asked herself again. This is perfectly innocent.

Later someone played the accordion and they joined in the dancing and then returned to the first table for some of Matilde's Easter gateau and more wine. By now Amy had convinced herself Davide would surely understand that she deserved a little light-hearted enjoyment.

'You two seemed to be having a lot of fun,' Giulia Nannini commented as they drove back to Rome.

'It was very nice,' said Amy, setting the afternoon firmly in the past.

'Giorgio is a decent person,' put in her husband. 'Respected in his field. I've read some of his essays.'

Amy thought the Nanninis sounded rather like matchmaking parents.

'I expect he is,' she said. 'But I'm feeling guilty now.'

Giulia looked over her shoulder and met her gaze. 'Guilty?'

'Because of Davide.'

The couple exchanged a glance. Giulia said: 'My dear Amy, I think you must realise that you'll probably never see him again. And from what you've told me, it's probably for the best. You're young, it's right you should enjoy yourself.'

******

'What a day we had yesterday!' Salvatore greeted her when she arrived at her spice stall the following morning. 'And what a monster of a headache I've got!'

'Serves you right for drinking all that wine,' Matilde looked up from unloading a crate of broad beans for her stall. She turned to Amy. 'You were certainly enjoying yourself, young lady.'

Amy murmured something. As she arranged her small packets of spices, the sky beyond her stall was blue and the sun surprisingly warm for April. She was thoughtful. A year had passed since her arrival in Rome, believing it to be for a short visit. Yet she was troubled by the mystery of Davide's mysterious career and his extended trips to Naples. He had never told her when he might return and during a particularly long absence last year she had considered her dilemma. Her friend, Paolo, asked her: 'what are you willing to lose if you stay here?' In spite of everything she was glad she had stayed and now felt firmly rooted in the city, but as the months had gone by so had her conviction faded they would meet again. If it wasn't for the occasional postcard, Davide might never have existed.

Thinking about the happy, uncomplicated day spent with Giorgio, Amy told herself that maybe Giulia was right, it was time to move on.

II

In the afternoon she climbed down the now familiar metal steps to the cat sanctuary. Above her, tourists teemed and traffic roared around the square but here there was comparative peace. She was glad to see that Susan, the squeaky voiced American, was on duty. There was no sign of Stephanie.

'She decided to *fare il ponte*,' Susan told her. 'She was off for the Easter weekend and it seems she's tacked on a more few days.'

Amy knew what her friend was thinking: how nice and relaxing it was without the Australian. They exchanged a smile then her friend's expression changed.

'Amy, I must tell you I haven't seen Shadow for the last twenty four hours.'

Shadow was the remarkable grey cat whose amber gaze had met hers the first time she had noticed there was a cat sanctuary at Largo Argentina. He was the feline who had launched her on such a surprising train of events.

'You know what he's like, answerable to no one. He'll probably show up today for food if he's hungry. Don't worry, Susan.'

'Oh but I do, I worry about them all. They rely on us.'

'And we don't let them down.'

Over time Amy had made an attempt to be more rational about these feral cats. Many arrived in a bad state of neglect or health and in spite of the best care they couldn't always be saved. Of course there were times when tears came to her eyes as their vet was forced to amputate a badly injured paw, or the infection that was rife among them made them lose their sight. Susan, on the other hand, appeared to have lost her former coping strategy and became increasingly emotional and anxious.

'Remember you once told me I shouldn't take everything to heart?' Amy said.

'I know, maybe I've been doing this too long. Nothing seems to change, does it? People still abuse animals or abandon them.'

Amy felt her previous cheerful mood dissipate. She gave the little woman a quick hug. 'Cheer up, let's get on with things.'

They went through the afternoon routine, cleaning out litter boxes, laying down fresh newspapers on the floor of the area where the better-behaved cats were allowed to roam. As always they paused to play with Mister Grumpy and his now constant companion, a small white cat.

'When you think how he used to hiss at us and lash out, I never thought he'd change. You did a wonderful job.' Susan's mood had lightened.

'You see, it's not all gloom and doom,' Amy was saying when someone spoke her name. Looking up she saw Concetta had arrived.

Standing there, dressed in her habitual old cardigan and drab skirt, she looked particularly frail today. '*Signore*, I have come on an urgent matter. Can we speak?'

In the small office area she sank onto a chair and brought her hands to her face. When she lowered them the two women were shocked by the distress in her gaze.

'A cat was found dead near Piazza del Popolo. It had been poisoned. That was the third this week.'

Silence followed while the others took this in, then Amy asked: 'how do you know they were poisoned?'

Concetta gave her a pitying look. 'Amy *cara*, I haven't been a *gattara* for over twenty years not to recognise when a cat has died that way.' She shook her head from side to side. 'It is a terrible, agonising death. Whoever is doing this is a monster.'

With a lurch of her heart Amy remembered Susan telling her she hadn't seen Shadow for some hours. She had a vision of someone throwing down poisoned meat, Shadow coming padding along, finding it, eating it. Please, not Shadow!

'We must do something about this,' she said. 'Have you gone to the police? Have you made a *denuncia*?'

'The police!' Concetta did an unexpected thing, she spat a gob of phlegm onto the ground. 'What do they care about our *mici*? Prancing about in their fancy capes, too busy helping pretty tourists.'

Amy exchanged a look with Susan. Concetta was old enough to remember the Italian Fascists of the Second World War and was well known for trusting no one who wore a uniform.

'So what do you want us to do?' she asked.

'Help me, help me track down this piece of shit before any more cats are killed.'

Susan murmured: 'Amy, I'd be careful if I were you.'

But meeting Concetta's pleading gaze, her eyes red rimmed from lack of sleep, she said: 'Yes, I'll help you. Where do we start?"

Two evenings later, Amy was standing by the great obelisk in Piazza del Popolo waiting for Concetta who was, as usual, late. They had agreed to start their hunt for the cat killer from the spot where the latest victim had been found. Seeing all the couples out enjoying the fine spring evening, she felt a flicker of loneliness.

It was all very well for Concetta, she was an old woman and her world centred round animals. Shouldn't she, Amy, be carefree like the groups of other young people she could see, meeting up for a fun evening out? She found herself thinking of Giorgio and wondered if she would see him again.

'Amy!' The cat lady had arrived beside her. 'How can you come out dressed like that? It's far too early in the year for such a thin jacket. At least you should wear a scarf!' She was dressed in a puffer coat with a knitted hat covering her grey hair.

'But it's so warm,' said Amy. She had heard about the fear of draughts, the *colpa d'aria* enough times. Giulia was forever warning her about their danger but she chose to ignore it.

Concetta grunted. 'After a year living here, young lady, you really should know better.'

Amy was gazing round the big square, which buzzed with the sound of voices as people met their friends or strolled. She couldn't imagine how they would track down the killer here.

'The cat wasn't found here,' Concetta replied. 'You know the road that leads up towards the Pincio Terrace? Somewhere along there.'

They crossed the square and, leaving the crowds behind, started up the tree- lined road. It was quieter here and only the occasional car passed.

Concetta halted and pointed into the undergrowth. 'It was somewhere here. I think there must be a small colony of cats nearby.'

Sure enough, after a short while, a ginger and white cat appeared but vanished the moment Concetta stooped to stroke it.

Amy was feeling at a loss. So, what do we do now?'

'Hang around? Wait until it's really dark. I have a torch.'

Half an hour later, Concetta gasped and clutched at Amy's arm. 'Look, look, over there.'

A man had appeared from the direction of the gardens. A little way ahead of them, he went down on his haunches calling '*micio, micio.*' He produced a paper bag and rustled it. Soon the ginger and white cat appeared followed by three others. The man emptied the contents of the bag onto the ground and at the same time Concetta pounced and kicked the food out of the animals' reach.

'What are you doing?' she shouted. 'How dare you harm those cats!'

The man leapt to his feet. '*Signora*, are you mad! He towered above the diminutive Concetta but she stood her ground.

'Who are you? What are you doing here?'

He laughed then. 'What I always do: Shut the café for the day. On my way out I feed these cats.' He turned to Amy. '*Signorina*, perhaps you should take your mother home, it must be past her bedtime.'

This remark only infuriated Concetta more. 'Show a bit more respect young man or I'll…'

'There's someone poisoning cats, you see,' Amy said. 'We're obviously worried but I'm sorry if we made a mistake.'

She recognised him now. He had served her on several occasions when she paused at the little kiosk pavilion near the garden's water clock. Surrounded by chestnut trees plane and oak, the building, La Casina dell'Orologio was a gem of 1920's architecture. On one occasion he had tempted her to try the classic Sicilian pastry, *cannoli*, but she had found it too rich.

'I have seen this too,' he said now. 'I am very worried.' He smiled. 'I suppose you could call me a part time *gattaro*.' He used the Italian name for a male cat lover.

Amy held out her hand. 'And we are *gattare*.'

They laughed and after a moment Concetta joined in.

III

A sudden shower of rain had Gian Franco unfurling their great umbrella. He and Giulia were on their way home from Sunday Mass at the church of Gertrude of Nivells. The rain lasted all the way back to their apartment where Giulia insisted they immediately don thick jumpers.

'We'll be lucky if we don't go down with something,' she muttered.

'We didn't even get wet,' her husband pointed out.

'It doesn't matter it's the atmosphere that is dangerous. *Colpo…*'

'*D'aria*,' finished Gian Franco. 'Yes, I know. But I think on this occasion we've escaped from being hit by air.'

Giulia resented the irony in his tone. She went into the kitchen to start preparing ingredients for lunch. Leonardo followed her, mewing piteously. He had shown no further wish for adventure since his escape from the apartment last year. That was his first encounter with the outside world, and he had spent several days on the streets before being kidnapped by Concetta, who was eventually forced by Davide to relinquish him. Leonardo now preferred to watch city life from the intervening windowpane, breaking off only to pick at the tasty morsels Giulia plied him with.

'That cat is becoming seriously overweight again,' Gian Franco remarked. 'Didn't *Dottore* Turiano say he should go on a diet?'

Giulia, busy in the kitchen, called: 'You can talk.'

He ignored this and, settling in his armchair, switched on the television. For a while last year Giulia had indulged his liking for the bosomy girls of Rete 4. This was after he had made his own small bid for freedom, accompanying his friend Antonio to a football match in Georgia. He had never let on to her that the exhausting days, as Antonio took him to what was possibly every bar in town, had made him long to be in his own bed. His absence had unnerved her and a different, sweeter Giulia had welcomed him home. Slowly however they had slipped back into the old squabbles.

Giulia came into the room carrying the aperitif they were allowed on the Sabbath. 'Father Eustachio wasn't his usual self this morning, did you not think?'

'I hadn't noticed. He seemed all right to me.'

'No, he definitely wasn't himself. He looked worried.' Giulia frowned. 'I hope he's not ill.'

'He's a born worrier.' Gian Franco's tone was vague as his favourite Selina Salerno appeared. She wore a dress that showed off her magnificent bosom to fine advantage. 'Take Father Bruno, he never seems to have a care in the world.'

'Too much levity isn't a good thing in a priest. He looks to me too fond of his stomach.'

'Nothing wrong with a man enjoying his food, priests are human like the rest of us.' His gaze had been drawn irresistibly back to the screen where Selina was planting a kiss on a winning contestant's cheek. Oh to be kissed by her!

Giulia's voice was stern. 'When you've had your fill, can I watch the weather?'

Reluctantly Gian Franco switched to Rai Uno and his wife's favourite weathercaster, the immaculately dressed colonel who proceeded to explain the chart in his precise Italian. It seemed that April this year was going to continue quite wet.

'We'll just have to be extra careful,' Giulia said

'That stuff Matilde served at *Pasquetta* was quite something, wasn't it?' Gian Franco remarked later as they sat down for lunch.

'Which, the *pasta alla Gricia*? Hmm I don't know where she buys her *guanciale* but I don't think it was a patch on mine!'

'Of course not,' Gian Franco hastily agreed. 'I suppose eating it in the open air makes it taste, well, different.'

'Different or better?'

'Just different.'

It being Sunday there were three courses. To start, Giulia had prepared artichokes *alla Romana* stuffed with garlic and wild mint then braised in olive oil and white wine.

'And that's another thing,' she said. 'Matilde doesn't use enough garlic. In fact, she told me she isn't keen on it, at all.'

Gian Franco ignored this, concentrating on the artichokes. Their buttery texture melted in the mouth. He poured their permitted second glass of wine.

A handsome sea bream followed the artichokes, which Gian Franco had borne proudly home from the market.

'I thought Amy looked really happy on Monday,' said Giulia while Gian Franco was engaged in extracting bones. The only drawback with fish, he thought.

'Yes, they looked good together.'

His wife sighed. 'I know. I said what I said because I felt I should. Between you and me, I still prefer Davide for all his mysterious life style. Well, he retrieved Leonardo for me, didn't he? And I know for a fact Giorgio doesn't like cats.'

'Oh? Who told you that?'

'The Englishwoman, *Signora* Russo, I met her the other day. Do you know, she still lets those children of hers run in the park without their jackets. And she must have lived here for five years. Anyway, she was at some charity do and spoke to his mother. She said he wouldn't harm them, of course, but he dislikes them because they hunt birds. What are you smiling at?' she asked.

'It just struck me. I don't know if Leonardo would know what to do if one sat on his nose.'

'You'd be surprised.' Giulia cleared the dishes and brought in the cheese board.

IV

Father Eustachio was deep in thought when his old friend Father Bruno arrived carrying a bulging string bag.

'Just a few little indulgences,' he said, unloading its contents. 'I think I'm allowed them today, don't you?'

April 21st was the priest's birthday, one he would gleefully point out he shared with the feast day of St Beuno, said to have performed many miracles including the restoration of St Winfred's head after she was martyred. Father Bruno had an impressive knowledge of Catholic saints even though, as he admitted, you couldn't account for all ten thousand of them.

Father Eustachio stared at the array of food with a sinking heart. He had very little appetite, even for the splendid strawberry gateau. All the same, he managed a smile and told himself he would not mention the events of last weekend on his friend's special day. He brought out the glasses and poured their favoured Barbera D'Asti. Father Bruno settled back in his chair with a contented sigh and took a sip.

'Nectar as always,' he said.

Father Eustachio raised his glass. 'Happy birthday, Bruno.'

They savoured the wine. Into his mind came an image of the scene that had met him on entering his church, last

Saturday. He thrust it away. 'How has your week been?' he asked.

'A spate of funerals,' his friend said cheerfully, 'one after the other. There was a single wedding. I told the bride you'd better get busy and make up the deficit.'

In spite of his preoccupation Father Eustachio had to laugh. 'You really are an old rascal, Bruno!'

The other grinned. 'You've got to keep your sense of humour in this job, old chap. Believe me there is a lot to laugh about. For example, I had this man come to me the other day who'd had his car stolen. He wanted me to say a novena for its recovery, I ask you.' He drained his glass and set it down.

Father Eustachio rose to refill it. Bruno's tale had put him in mind of *Signora* Nannini's request for a novena when her ginger cat went missing. And this brought him back to the incident, which was troubling him. Early on Saturday morning he had gone into the church to supervise the flowers for the afternoon's wedding and sensed that someone had been there before him. He walked towards the altar, glancing nervously left and right to the side chapels until he came to the statue of Gertrude of Nivells. Horrified he saw it had been vandalised. The face of the patron saint of cats had been sprayed with red paint, which had trickled down over her sculpted cape and dress onto the cat on her lap. Much as he disliked cats and this woman's connection with them, believing them agents of the devil, the sight shocked him.

Who could have done this? When? But there was no time for these questions, so when Luciano, the altar server, entered the church he grabbed him by the arm.

'Quickly help me! Fetch that shawl from the vestry now.'

The startled Luciano obeyed and the statue was swiftly wrapped. Father Eustachio felt very angry and was shocked by a desire for vengeance.

A slice of strawberry gateau was put in front of him. Father Eustachio eyed it.

'Come on, my friend,' Father Bruno had been watching him. 'There is something on your mind, It's plain to see. Spill the beans.'

'I didn't want to spoil your birthday.'

Father Bruno shrugged. 'Nothing could spoil it when I am drinking this excellent wine.'

He related the tale of vandalism, finishing: 'If I'm honest, I want to find that person who did such a senseless thing and beat him up!'

His friend wagged his finger. 'No, no, that's not the attitude you should take, understandable of course but no. Don't hold on to anger, old chap, for your own sake. When you can't forgive someone you hurt yourself. That person, whoever it was, will move on and you'll be left holding onto the frustration and pain. It's difficult but if you can bring yourself to forgive you will be set free.'

On the Sunday, Father Eustachio spoke of forgiveness borrowing freely from the text of Psalm 103.

Nevertheless, all the time he was aware of the shawled statue in her shadowy side chapel. He prayed that none of the congregation would notice and start gossiping. The Lord might be slow to anger, but his own would be in danger of boiling over.

V

Concetta seemed capable of existing on only a few hours of sleep. 'Whatever time I go to bed, I'm usually up by five.'

Amy on the other hand needed her eight hours and so, after yet another fruitless night seeking the poisoner near Piazza del Popolo, she suggested they had a break. It was like looking for a needle in a haystack, she pointed out, unless they had other clues. Even so, she arrived an hour late to set up her stall and was greeted by Matilde.

'Oh, here you are. Someone was looking for you earlier. I think it was the young man you were with at *Pasquetta*.'

'Giorgio! Oh no! Did he leave any message?'

'He said he was on his way to work and would come back tomorrow.'

As she arranged her samples of Mexican chilli, her offering for tastings that morning, she found she was unreasonably excited. He was probably only coming out of curiosity, she told herself. When she had described her mother's shop *Zest* in England and how she had discovered she had a 'nose' for the spices he'd found it amusing.

'I've heard of a 'nose' for perfumes but this is a novelty. I have the odd curry now and again but I can't say it's my favourite food.'

'Oh there is so much more to cooking with spices,' Amy spoke earnestly, 'a whole culinary world, in fact. I never stop learning.'

'I'm intrigued to know more,' he had said.

Now he was coming to find out. Amy hummed to herself as she put a little fork into each taster dish. Salvatore arrived as always, bearing a tray on which sat two espresso.

'You're in a good mood,' he said.

Why shouldn't I be? The sun is shining and I have three big orders from restaurants. I seem to have created quite a stir.'

The small Sicilian regarded her for a moment. 'It wouldn't be anything to do with a certain young man?'

Amy blushed, a reaction she'd always hoped she'd grow out of. 'Honestly, you two! You're so nosy. I can't make a move without your finding out.'

Salvatore drained his small cup. 'It isn't true. We care about you, that's all.'

She smiled. 'I know and it's lovely. You're all so kind.'

Paolo was the first person she had met in Rome, and he had quickly become a dear friend. He was the brother of Marco who had held a lifelong love for Amy's mother, following their doomed affair. Paolo's advice and support had helped her through her darker days when she had debated leaving Rome. She had arranged to meet him for an aperitif that evening and would sound him out about Giorgio.

They met in *L'Angelo Divino*, a small rustic wine bar tucked away in a side street near Campo de Fiori. Amy arrived first and was gazing at the huge number of wine bottles that lined the walls when she heard her name. As always Paolo was immaculate, dressed tonight in a dark blue jacket and jeans. He looked much younger than his fifty-seven years.

'Amy *cara*, I apologise for being late. I had a call from France just as I was about to leave and I had to talk to my friend. Shall we have a plate of cheese and cold meats to go with our wine? I didn't have time for lunch.' He signalled to the waiter who immediately brought a bottle to their table. Paolo declined to taste it before it was poured.

'They know what I like,' he said. 'I often come here away from prying eyes.' Amy thought that, although being gay was now accepted without question, he seemed to continue to fear the prejudices of the time when he was young.

'So how's life?' he asked.

'Fine, the spices are going really well, at last. And we have the most adorable new tabby cat at Largo Argentina.'

'I meant your personal life.' He smiled. 'Isn't there something you want to tell me?'

She was always impressed by his intuitive nature. Amy blushed.

'Now I know there *is* something.'

She took up her glass, set it down again. 'I think I've met someone.'

'Only think?'

'I've only seen him once but he's nice. We get on really well and,' she smiled, 'he's coming to check out my stall tomorrow.'

'So, you're finally over Davide?'

Amy felt the familiar ache at the mention of his name. 'I'll never be 'over' Davide, but it's no use, is it? I've lost hope that I'll see him again. I have to be sensible.'

Paolo forked some cheese and salami onto his plate. 'Being sensible is not easy in affairs of the heart, I know. But I wouldn't want you to become like Marco.'

She sipped her wine, thinking of the Protestant cemetery where he was buried, the inscription on his gravestone…*a heart breaking can be as quiet as a feather falling. No one hears it but you.* There had been times when she felt exactly like that.

'I have to live,' she appealed.

'Of course, it is quite right that you do. I don't suppose I know him, do I? I'm acquainted with so many families in Rome.'

The wine bar was filling up as people started to arrive after work. She had to raise her voice to reply. 'Giorgio Bevacqua.'

She was surprised by Paolo's wary reaction. 'He's not an archaeologist, by any chance?'

She nodded, her mouth full of the delicious anti pasto.

'Clever young man, I've read his work in *Archaeologia*.' His expression altered. 'I've nothing against Giorgio but he comes from a rather strange family.'

'Strange?'

Paolo was silent for a moment.

'Paolo?'

His dark eyes met hers. He reached over and patted her hand. 'Take no notice of me, Amy. I'm just being silly. Enjoy yourself. It's time you did.'

Later Amy sat at the big window of the apartment that was now her home. Behind her the lamp gleamed on the patina of the old tiled floor, and the sofa where she and Davide had kissed was in shadow. The room seemed to have lost the melancholy she had sensed when she first came here. As she had lived in it and made it her own, it had become her haven. She gazed down onto the square beyond where the evening crowds strolled or stood in groups to talk. She loved this city and told herself she should be grateful that life had brought her here and offered the chance to remain. She longed to share it with someone and had thought it would be Davide until he told her he had no idea when they would see each other again. Now Giorgio had arrived. No need to get involved, just enjoy, as Paolo had said. But he had also said the

Bevacqua family was strange. What had he meant? And why had he changed his mind about explaining further?

VI

It was Giulia's turn to hear about the cat killer. Since she had met Amy and revealed her own part in the story of Marco and Caroline, she had taken to volunteering at Largo Argentina.

'Not every day,' she had said. 'Leonardo would miss me too much.' And Gian Franco might see it as an opportunity to meet up with his friend Antonio, she added silently.

Neither was she prepared to do the day-to-day work of cleaning and feeding. 'I'd rather be the upfront person, talk to visitors and persuade them to donate.' This proved to be her forte and scarcely anyone escaped without handing over some lire.

'Street cats die from all kinds of diseases,' she said when Susan told her of the continuing deaths. 'Poor things, but who told you they'd been poisoned?'

'The *gattara* of Piramide, Concetta.'

'The woman who kidnapped my cat! She's a stupid, hysterical creature, how can you believe a word she says?' She remembered the day she and her husband had joined with Amy and her friend Davide to rescue Leonardo. 'She had the audacity to rename him *Amara. Amara*, I ask you!'

Susan's eyes were steely behind her granny glasses. 'Unfortunately, it seems she's right. Our vet has done an autopsy on some of them. They were definitely poisoned.'

'I see. I presume you have made a *denuncia*?'
Reporting to the police was Giulia's weapon against the injustices of this world. The fact that often there were no apparent results did nothing to deter her.

'No, not yet. Concetta thinks it would be a waste of time.'

'Hmm, Concetta.'

She spent the afternoon brooding on this and took it out on the visitors, extracting 50 lire from one of them, much to Stephanie's delight. The Australian said she found Giulia to be a woman after her own heart.

At five when the cats were being fed, including the elusive Shadow who, to Amy's relief had shown himself, Giulia was able to slip away.

Sunshine had brought the crowds onto the streets. She pushed her way through them and crossed to Piazza Venezia near to where 'her' police station was situated. The front office was empty so she sat down to wait. After a while a police officer appeared from the street carrying a cup of coffee and a plastic bag. Giulia sprang to her feet.

'I want to report...' she hesitated over the word 'murders' then continued: 'some criminal behaviour.'

The policeman, a middle-aged man with a weary expression on his face, set his shopping down behind the counter.

'Yes madam, certainly madam.'

He went into the back office and returned with a *denuncia* form, which Giulia knew very well. Over the years, she had delivered them on several occasions, the last relating to the kidnap of Leonardo when a much younger officer had reacted in surprise saying cats were not his remit. This officer cast a longing look at his coffee.

Giulia smiled. 'Don't worry, I'll do it.'

He sat down on his chair with a sigh, took up the cup and sipped while she filled in her personal details. When she came to the description of the crime she paused. She had no idea where the dead cats had been found nor who the killer was. She wrote: *a person or persons unknown is poisoning this city's cats*. There was a pause while the officer read it. He looked up and Giulia was startled by his expression.

'There is a law that bans the killing of stray cats and protects them. They should be allowed to live without disruption in the place where they were born. My aunt Lucia is a *gattara* and we have adopted two ginger female cats.'

'Ginger!' Giulia exclaimed. 'My Leonardo is ginger. But they are usually male, are they not?'

'Yes, I'm told it's something to do with the X chromosome.'

'Really, I didn't know that.'

They were off, discussing the merits of sandy coloured felines. The *denuncia* lay on the counter forgotten until Giulia drew his attention to it.

'Leave it with me,' he said.

As she made her way home, a thought came into her mind. Marco would have been proud of me.

VII

1966 GIULIA

If Rome of the 1960s saw an explosion of style and glamour and, of course, the cinema at Cinecitta, the so called, Hollywood on the Tiber, Giulia was excluded. Her mother forbade her to go anywhere near the Via Veneto. The 'outlandish behaviour' in its bars, nightclubs and restaurants made it no place for a young girl, she said. And as for Taylor and Burton shamelessly carrying on for everyone to see, that was disgraceful. Giulia longed to go to see Pink Floyd at the Piper disco, to dance the Mashed Potato, the Hitchhiker and the Watsusi, as many of her friends were doing.

'Out of Africa,' her mother said. 'All that wiggling about is unfeminine and ungainly. Whatever happened to the waltz and the quickstep, partnered by a nice young man?'

Giulia murmured: '*Che palle!*'

'For the love of God, where did you learn that?'

'Papa says it.'

'I know and I dislike it, but coming from you…*e ripugnante*'

In her room, Giulia eyed herself in the mirror, admiring her long dark hair, her full lips and slender body. Look at me, she thought, I should be out having fun. I will become a fat old matron before I have lived, because of my stupid mother. She wasn't a child anymore, nearly twenty for heaven's sake.

So that when Marco asked her out, she felt her life had at last begun. She had admired him since middle school, his good looks, and his confidence that life was to be seized upon. He seemed to Giulia so sophisticated in the way he behaved. As they moved on to secondary school, he was among the first to own a Vespa. Part of this self-assurance was due to the fact he came from a well-off family... the Giordano clan had made their money as jewellers, whereas the Altavillas were modest in comparison. Nevertheless, there came the day when he stopped his Vespa when she was walking home from school and asked if she would like a ride.

She stared at him in disbelief. Marco Giordano had noticed her.

He laughed. 'Well hop on then, unless you're afraid.'

She shook her head, not trusting herself to speak and climbed on behind him. He shouted above the engine she should hold on. They careered through the streets as far as St Peter's and then back to the historic centre. As she leant against him, she felt it was the happiest day of her life.

She didn't tell her mother but *Signora* Altavilla looked suspicious. 'Your hair is all over the place,' she said. 'What have you been up to?'

'Nothing, Mamma.'

'Go to your room and make yourself respectable before your father comes home.'

A few days later, Marco asked her if she would like to go to the cinema. 'There's a good film on I'd like to see.'

It was a spaghetti western that centred on the tricks, deceits, unexpected actions and sarcasm of the hero, but it could have been Fellini's most bewildering work for all the notice Giulia took of it. The nearness of Marco and the smell of his cologne made her feel breathless. She wondered if he would hold her hand but he didn't, not on that evening and not for several after that. But he took her to the *Caffe Antico della Pace* in Piazza Navona and they sat at an outdoor table overlooking the splendid square. Giulia gazed in wonder at the crowds from all over the world as they strolled before the church of *Santa Maria della Pace*. She felt she had finally broken loose from her mother's control and when Marco offered her a cigarette she accepted and smoked for the first time in her life.

VIII

A few days after her conversation with Paolo, Amy was washing up her supper things when the phone rang. For some weeks she had rushed to answer it, thinking it would be Davide. Now she took her time peeling off her rubber gloves before she lifted the receiver.

'Darling, it's me. I tried you the other evening but you were out. I hope you were enjoying yourself.'

'I was having an aperitif with Paolo, Mum.'

'Paolo? Oh, so nothing special. Listen,' she went on, 'I've some exciting news. Your cousin is getting married.' Her mother laughed. 'Annette's really landed a catch.'

Amy pictured her tall, blonde cousin who had had a string of boyfriends, all discarded because they did not, in her eyes, come up to scratch.

'Good for her.'

'Such a nice young man,' her mother was saying. 'Has his own accountancy firm. They've bought a beautiful house in Richmond.'

Amy was silent.

'Amy, are you still there?'

'Yes.'

'We were wondering, your father and I, whether you'd want to come home for the wedding? It's in September. All the family will be there.'

Unless Annette finds something wrong with him, meanwhile, Amy thought. He must be a real doormat to deal with her. What a cynic you've become, she scolded herself.

'It got me thinking,' came her mother's voice. 'Why couldn't it have been you getting married? I'd have loved helping you choose your dress and organising your reception. Such a pity! You know, if you came back to England I'm sure you'd find someone nice.'

There was a pause in which Amy remained silent.

Her mother's tone changed. 'You really ought to start thinking about your future, Amy. You're not a teenager anymore.'

'And I'm not old either, Mum. Anyway, I don't want to leave Rome. I'm happy here.'

She heard the familiar sound of her mother inhaling smoke. Saw in her mind's eye the scallop shell near the phone that Caroline used as an ashtray.

'So you say. Darling, we hardly see you. Your father was saying, only the other day, apart from those few days over Christmas you've not been home for a year.'

To change the subject Amy enquired after Zest, the spice business was now nearly eight years old.

'Fine darling, it's going fine. But I have to admit it's not the same without you.'

Amy felt a pang of guilt, remembering her mother's expression when she'd said goodbye directly after New Year.

'Why's that?' she asked.

'You were such an asset. The customers loved you and you were always coming up with new ideas.'

It was true, she had. With a touch of nostalgia she remembered how, in the early days of Zest, she discovered her special sensitivity to the aroma of spices, and that this led her to devise original blends, often tailored to a particular customer. She had been an asset with her 'nose', one her mother lacked.

'I was thinking if you came back to England,' Caroline's voice was wistful, 'we'd set you up with your own shop. You wouldn't even have to live in the same town as us if you didn't want to. It would just be lovely to have you nearby.'

Amy put down the receiver feeling unsettled as she often did after one of these conversations with her mother. She knew she could have had the life her cousin was about to embark on if she had stayed with Stephen. He had a 'safe' job in the local estate agents and would have provided generously for her. He had said as much. She also knew she had done the right thing in ending their relationship. They held different views on many things, which hadn't seemed to matter at first, until she began to talk about doing some travelling before she could even think of settling down. She remembered his reaction: "So you've been leading me on, kidding me you were serious about us when you just want to flit around the world!"

She had promised herself she would stay clear of any involvement while in Rome. After all, this was her opportunity to strike out on her own, away from her mother's over-protectiveness, to have new experiences and discover more about herself. Then she had met Davide and, for a while, believed her future lay with him. Giorgio hadn't returned to Campo de Fiori as he'd told Matilde he would. Tonight, watching the couples pass beneath the window, she wished that, if it were not meant to be Davide, there would be someone special to share her life.

Rain fell all through the night. Each time she woke she lay and listened to the gentle, steady downpour. It seemed to echo her mood as she made her way to Campo de Fiore to set out her stall.

'What weather!' Salvatore greeted her as he arrived with his tray bearing their customary espresso. A creature of the sun, he looked miserable and bedraggled. They sipped and he gave her a wry smile. 'We could be in England.'

Soon the square was bobbing with umbrellas as the morning shoppers arrived, several of them not stopping to examine the stalls but to make their way to the little bakery on the corner. From here they emerged with slices of pizza as well as the daily bread.

As the morning progressed the rain slackened, the sun broke through and a rainbow arched across the sky. Still no one approached Amy's stall. She gazed at the spectrum of colour until it faded and the rain stopped. She remembered her mother's words. *Where will you be in five years time? Ten? You won't be young forever, you need to think about your future.* Time passed slowly while on either side, Matilde and Salvatore were now busy serving customers. She was just planning to pack up early and go to her favourite café in Piazza Farnese when someone said her name. A tall, broad shouldered man had arrived at her stall. It was Giorgio.

He laughed at her surprise. 'Sorry I didn't come the other day. I was called away to advise the police about antiquities that had been seized from some warehouses.' He frowned. 'There's been so much looting going on, you'd never believe.'

'How awful,' she said.

'I know, beautiful Etruscan vases they sell off to the United States. It's a huge trade. Do you know, some of them still had the dirt on them.'

She remembered his smile, his relaxed manner. It seemed natural to slip back into the effortless conversation they'd had at *Pasquetta*.

'Anyway, it's all sorted now.' He turned his attention to her stall. 'So, show me some of your favourite spices.'

She breathed a silent sigh of relief she had not started to pack them up. Grains of Paradise made him laugh when she explained how Salvatore had bought them for their name, not realising how hot they were. She chose not to add the tale of Giulia's mistake with curry powder then finished: 'I can offer you a taster of today's specialty?'

'It sounds good but how about having a bite to eat with me? If you have the time, of course.'

'That would be lovely.' How strange it was, she thought, I'm not gabbling and saying silly things as I did when Davide first asked me out. I wonder why that is?

Giorgio even had a chat with Matilde while Amy hastily stowed the packages away into her big holdall. She heard him complimenting her on the spread she'd provided for the festivities. As they strolled away across the piazza, he shouldering her holdall, she turned to look back and Salvatore gave her a thumbs-up.

Il Delfino was packed but they found a table. Giorgio returned from the counter and unloaded a tray of pizza slices, French fries and beer.

'Is that enough?' he asked. 'I'm not one for a big Roman lunch, are you?'

Amy shook her head. She bit into her slice and the filling oozed down her chin. Somehow she didn't feel embarrassed, as she might have done with Davide. But then Davide never brought her to a *tavola calda* like this one. He was always impeccably dressed even when they went to the lakes, unlike…she eyed Giorgio's casual shirt, the red, horn-shape charm he wore round his neck. Why did she keep on comparing one with the other, Amy asked herself, what was she trying to prove?

Giorgio was asking how she had come to live in Rome.

She told him something about Marco and her mother Caroline's failed affair.

'It's so sad because it seems they were deeply in love.'

He drank from his cardboard cup. 'So what happened?'

'His mother ruined it all. She wanted her son to marry an Italian woman and she set out to get rid of Mum.'

'Mm, yes, Italian mothers can be pretty powerful. I'm lucky, mine is American and easy going.'

Amy was thinking of the grave in the Protestant Cemetery, the tragic inscription on Marco's headstone.

'He never forgot her, you see, never really loved again. His brother told me he believes Marco died of a broken heart. I don't know about my mother though. She's never wanted to visit Rome and she didn't want the apartment Marco left her in his will.' She finished the last of her fries. 'Which is where I live now.'

Giorgio reached over and took her hand.'

'The good thing is, it's brought you to Rome, don't you agree?'

She gazed at their joined hands and then up to his face. He was watching her, waiting for her answer. He really likes me, she thought and the doubts she'd had since the conversation with her mother faded. 'Yes,' she said.

IX

A Roman dawn: the first sunrays have a special quality, they seem to be absorbed rather than reflected and the very white stones of the monument to King Victor Emanuel profits from this occurrence. Later on in full daylight it will take the appearance of a sugar coated wedding cake. Nightclubs spew their last revellers who blink and stagger into the deserted streets. One figure detaches itself and makes off into the Parco Colle Oppio where once he was disturbed. He scatters the contents of a plastic bag over the ground and with a hollow laugh gropes his way towards the exit, hanging on to any convenient tree.

There is a small colony of cats nearby and the majority are wary of these dawn visits but there is one young curious feline that dares to approach this bounty of food. She is thin and hungry. Often, the older cats bat her away and take all the food given by their gattare. But now is her chance and she gobbles with greed.

A few minutes later the provider of food is rewarded by the desperate cries of a cat seized by the agonising pain of rodent poisoning. Her screams rend the violet air, sounds that would halt the hardest heart in its tracks, but not his. He glories in it. He delights in inflicting pain and these animals have become the focus of his hatred. Now he can resume his wanderings of the city in search of more victims.

Gradually the sun's rays reach the lower parts of Rome. For some time the buildings to the west of the seven hills are still in darkness while their domes and loggias are already bathed in sunshine. There is no one about. This is the time he likes best, unseen, unheard he goes about his self-appointed task.

******

Father Eustachio, taking his morning coffee, riffled through the pages of *Il Messaggero* until a headline caught his eye. "Mystery assassin of Rome's cats." The article went on to state that the city council supported the cats as a part of Rome's ancient heritage.

"In antiquity, the cat was highly valued for defending mankind against rodent-borne diseases like the plague and was even worshipped by some sects of Ancient Rome, a tradition brought over from the neighbouring Egyptian Empire."

Postcards portraying the felines were bought in thousands by tourists, every year. An eyewitness who wouldn't be named said he'd glimpsed a tall, well-made man lurking near the site where the latest victims had been discovered. "Police admit they are baffled," it concluded.

49

At that moment the telephone rang. It was Father Bruno. For once his tone was subdued. 'Good morning, have you seen the piece in today's *Il Messaggero* about the cats?'

`I'm reading it now.'

'Frankly I'm worried, old chap. I know you're not a lover of them but I'm concerned for my little lot over here in Trastevere.'

Father Eustachio forced himself to make sympathetic noises. He disliked cats as he disliked most animals ever since being bitten by his mother's Pekinese as a child.

'And not only that,' his friend continued. 'I was remembering what happened to that statue in your church, the one of St Gertrude of Nivells. She is the patron saint of cats so this could be connected. Is there some maniac out there with a hatred of animals?'

Father Eustachio stiffened. This certainly put a different complexion on things. The image of a madman entering his church was frightening. What if he had been there? What else was this person capable of?

'Why don't I pop over this evening, if you're free?' came Father Bruno's voice. 'We could discuss what we should do.'

Later that morning, Father Eustachio went over to his church to check on St Gertrude's statue. The incident had been reported to the police and the disfiguring scarlet paint removed. He paused to stare at the figure of the young woman. Her carved head was covered by a wimple and veil from which a length of braided hair escaped. Her face was attractive in a contemporary way, lips parted in a smile that showed her teeth. She cradled a large cat. For once he felt a sense of ownership. Her church was in his care, after all, he had a duty to protect. There came the sound of footsteps and he glanced round nervously. No, it was just an elderly woman who was now settling herself in a pew. He turned back to the statue and read its inscription. *I will not leave you comfortless.*

He crossed himself, murmuring: 'Father protect us from evil', nodding to the woman as he left the church.

******

An emergency meeting had been called at the cat sanctuary. By the time Amy arrived, a little late after her lunch with Giorgio, the others were all assembled: Susan, Stephanie and by consent, Concetta. Only Giulia was absent. 'It's her husband's sister's birthday,' it was explained. No one said anything about her antipathy for Concetta. A copy of *Il Messaggero* lay on the table, open at the article about cats.

Susan was unashamedly weeping. 'Five' she murmured, 'five of them in one night. Those poor beautiful babies how they must have suffered.' She raised her tear stained face. 'You've never seen a poisoned cat, Amy. It's terrible, terrible and they don't die quickly, it's a slow and agonising death.' She drummed her fists on the table. 'I'd like to tear this man from limb to limb. I'd like to force him to take the same poison. Bastard!'

'Calm yourself, Susan,' Stephanie took control. 'What good is screaming and shouting going to do? You'll make yourself ill.'

'What do I care? It's those poor little souls, I'm thinking of.' Susan fell into another outburst of grief.

Amy looked on, feeling helpless. Stephanie was right of course but she could understand Susan's outpouring. It was true she had never witnessed a cat poisoning but she could use her imagination to picture the ghastly scene. She fetched the box of tissues, which was always handy and went down on her haunches to speak quietly to the anguished American woman.

Above her Stephanie was speaking. 'Sooner or later this man is going to poison one of our cats, unless he's caught. In fact we don't even know if he's already been here among the visitors.'

'Ah!' Concetta held up her hand. 'At least we have a clue.' She stabbed the newspaper with a finger. 'A witness said he was tall and well-built.'

Amy sighed. 'But you can't suspect every man that looks like that.'

'It's a start.'

'So we have to be wary of all the tall, well-built men who come here.'

There was a pause.

Stephanie said: 'We'll have to make sure every cat is inside before we lock up for the night.'

Shadow, Amy thought. Her beautiful grey cat with the amber eyes, that often disappeared among the ruins. No one could control Shadow.

She turned to Concetta. 'Perhaps we should go out in the evenings again, but where? He could be anywhere in Rome.'

They arranged to meet up next day.

Susan recovered sufficiently to go back to work and the meeting broke up. Concetta left for her colony at Piramide, to give her cats their evening meal.

Amy went in search of Shadow and found him sunning himself in his favourite spot on a fallen piece of masonry. She sat by him to stroke his luxuriant fur and he started to purr. Over the time she had worked at Largo Argentina he had become her confidante, seeming to understand her every mood. Today it was one of exhilaration, which even the cat murders couldn't subdue.

As they'd stood outside *Il Delfino*, loathe to part it seemed, though both were busy that afternoon, Giorgio had asked when he would see her again.

'Have you ever been to Villa Giulia?' he asked. 'It houses the National Etruscan Museum. It's well worth a visit if you haven't.'

They arranged he would pick her up the following Saturday.

'We could drive up to the Aventine Hill afterwards,' Giorgio suggested. 'There's a fantastic view over the city you'll love.'

Yes, Amy thought, I know that view. I stood there with Davide, at the end of our first date and longed for him to kiss me.

Giorgio's gaze had lingered over her and he seemed about to say something else. He shrugged. 'It will keep. *A presto*, Amy.' He leaned forward and kissed her on both cheeks.

'He's nice,' she told the cat. 'Very nice and so uncomplicated.' Unlike Davide, she thought. She would never stop thinking of him, however hard she tried. The short time they had spent together was indelibly printed on her mind.

'Remember I love you,' he had said on their last night together. It was becoming more difficult to remember or believe that, the longer he was away.

X

Settled in Father Eustachio's study, sipping the wine merchant's latest recommendation, an inky coloured, deliciously silky *Nero D'Avola*, the two priests concluded their rather fruitless discussion about the cat poisoner.

'We could offer a novena?' Father Bruno suggested. 'After all, your novena to St Rita of Cascia produced results.'

His friend recalled the prayers he'd been persuaded to say to the saint of impossible causes for the recovery of the vanished cat, Leonardo.

'Worth a try, I suppose.'

Father Bruno's attention was diverted to the wine. 'This is an interesting little number. The aroma suggests a red that's fresh and floral with some spicy hints. But when you sip you realise there's far more to this wine. It leaves a nice grippy feel in the mouth.'

'*Nebbiolo*, yes it can be very deceptive.'

For a moment they sipped and dwelt on this elusive quality and then Father Eustachio changed the subject to broach his plan.

'How do you fancy a trip to some sacred sites? I've been hoarding the City Pilgrimages leaflet for some time and it suddenly seems a good idea to have a little respite.'

'Ordinarily I'd say yes but there are my cats, I'd be worried about them.'

'Wouldn't Anna keep an eye on them?'

Father Bruno considered the qualities of his elderly housekeeper. 'I suppose so. She is something of a *gattara*.'

'There you are then,' Father Eustachio leant over to refill his friend's glass. 'Come on Bruno, it's not like you to turn down a jaunt out of town. It will do you good to get away.'

The other stared into the depths of the ruby coloured liquid in his glass as if he were consulting the oracle. 'All right, if it's just for a few days.'

'Friday to Monday and we'd better hurry to book. There are only a few seats left.'

The excursion to visit the sacred sites of Loreto and Mannoppello was all-inclusive. They would travel by special coach with the other pilgrims to stay at the Hotel Angelica and take all their meals together. This last detail slightly alarmed Father Eustachio who liked his own space but it was one Father Bruno found particularly attractive.

What neither of them had accounted for was the presence of Sister Assunta, a hawk nosed nun, who boarded the coach accompanied by the younger and timid Sister Veronica. It was clear from the start that the older nun had appointed herself as the expert on this trip. She had been on previous pilgrimages and continually corrected their guide as they bowled through the ever more green countryside towards the east coast and Le

Marche. 'No it was built later than that, in the sixth century' 'Not Art Nouveau it's Art Deco.'

The two priests exchanged an anxious glance. Were they in for three days of this?

The *Angelica* appeared to be a relic of the 1960s, carpeted throughout in a swirly orange. They were shown to rooms so sparsely furnished their hosts appeared to be sticking to the letter of the vow of poverty. After a quick wash and brush up, Father Eustachio joined Father Bruno in the corridor

'If this is an indication, whatever will dinner be like?' he sighed.

'At least we can have some wine.'

What the meal lacked in quality it certainly made up for in quantity. Great bowls of pasta were set in front of them, topped with a few spoonsful of tomato sauce. A slab of unidentifiable meat followed this unprepossessing starter, served with boiled potatoes and carrots.

'You'd think we were in England,' Father Bruno murmured.

Dessert consisted of an overripe pear and a very small bunch of grapes.

'My God in heaven!' Father Eustachio slammed down his napkin. 'Three days of enduring this! Even the wine tastes as if it's been watered down.'

From the other side of the table Sister Assunta had been watching them. 'Enjoying your dinner, monsignors?' She asked.

'Hardly.'

'We are not here for a jolly outing.' The nun looked disapprovingly. 'This is a pilgrimage remember, not an excuse for indulgence.'

Sister Veronica stifled a giggle.

Sister Assunta rose to her full height and stood over them like an avenging harpy. 'I'll bid you goodnight.' She stared at the half empty bottle. 'I wouldn't have too much more of that. We have an early start in the morning.'

It was while they stood in the heart of the Mary House sanctuary, listening to the guide recount the miraculous carriage to Loreto of her humble dwelling by flights of angels, that two tourists joined them. Sister Assunta was too occupied with pouncing on any inaccuracy she believed the guide was making to notice, but then a murmured 'infiltrators' caught her attention. She advanced on the pair with an imperious gesture, and ordered them to leave.

'Oh please, can't we just hear the end? It was so interesting. My daughter is studying the Marian cult for her degree.'

'Go!' ordered the stern nun.

As they walked away and the group turned its attention back to the guide, Father Bruno hurried after them. As if from a magician's hat, he produced two of the blue and white neck scarves worn by everyone on a City Pilgrimages tour.

'Just say you got lost from another group.'

At the end of the morning, the 'infiltrators' approached the two priests with an invitation to lunch.

It was with pleasure they slipped away with the two women, who knew of a typical trattoria off the beaten track. The meal was a triumph of local specialties. *Tagliatelle* with the white truffle of Acqualagna was followed by a hearty main course. The wine they drank, a crisp *Verdicchio*, was equally delicious. While they ate, they regaled the two women with the behaviour of Sister Assunta and the terrible dinner they'd endured the night before.

'You poor dears,' Joan, the mother said. 'We've been to Le Marche several times but never had food like that.' She turned to her daughter. 'What do you think, Izzy? Shouldn't these two gentlemen move to our hotel?'

The audacity of this suggestion, the thought of flouting Sister Assunta's authority shocked Father Eustachio. But his friend had no such qualms. 'What a wonderful idea.'

They were late in re-joining the group for the afternoon visit, having stopped by the hotel to book their rooms. They were met by a disapproving silence.

'Most inconsiderate, we almost went without you,' said Sister Assunta.

They didn't care. Throughout the afternoon they hugged their secret to themselves, savouring the thought of more delicious food that night.

XI

Davide's name was mentioned two days later when Amy was having lunch with Paolo. When he'd called her, his voice had sounded hesitant.

'I was wondering whether you'd like to meet up, if you have the time?'

Privately, she'd been avoiding him since he had made the remark about Giorgio's family.

'May I buy you lunch?' he was asking. 'I thought we'd go back to that place you like, the *Basile*.'

May was in full swing and the air warm and scented with flowers from the street traders' stalls. She took the now familiar route crossing Ponte Sisto to enter the small streets and lanes of Trastevere. She'd planned to pass by the little church of St Michael to say hello to Father Bruno's cats. The iron gates were slightly ajar and she stepped through into the courtyard garden where a fountain softly played amidst rosebushes. Unlike a previous visit when she had heard the splendid tones of an organ, all was silent within the church. She waited a while, hoping the cats would appear but none came. She prayed it was because it was early and the priest was still to arrive and feed them. As she stood there, hesitating as to whether to enter the church, she remembered the strange experience she'd had, the year before, as she stood before the mosaic of a six-winged elaborately plumed angel. There had come an overwhelming sense of certainty that she loved Davide and all would be well if she clung to hope. She felt an ache of longing to see his face again, followed by the resignation that he had resumed his other life, whatever that was. The tinkle of the fountain seemed now to mock her. After another few moments she turned her back on the garden and made her way to the *Basile*.

Paolo rose from the table as she arrived. He looked tanned and fit, newly returned from one of his frequent trips to the South of France. He seemed delighted to see her, raising his glass of Kir Royale in welcome.

'Before we order, I have a little present for you.'

She removed the brown paper wrapping then stared in surprise as a book was revealed.

'You've read it?' He had misinterpreted her silence.

'How strange,' she murmured, eyeing the title, *The Garden of the Finzi-Continis*. 'I haven't, but Mum has. She was reading it about the time she met Marco.'

It was his turn to murmur: 'How strange.'

The wine arrived and Paolo filled their glasses. 'How is your mother?' he asked.

Amy grimaced. 'Still on at me to go back to England.'

'And you're never tempted? It worries me sometimes to think of you on your own in that apartment.'

'But I'm not alone. I have friends and now I have Giorgio.'

'Ah yes, Giorgio.'

They turned their attention to the menu and Amy chose the dish she'd enjoyed before: homemade ravioli stuffed with ricotta and served with aubergine, tomatoes and olives.

While they waited, Paolo brought up the subject of Giorgio again. 'Have you met the family yet?'

She had to smile at his anxious expression. 'Of course not, we're just friends, we see each other now and again.'

'That's good.'

What did he mean? Better that they stayed that way and the relationship didn't develop further? She decided not to pursue it, and he said no more. But long after they'd said goodbye, his enigmatic remarks continued to worry at her.

XII

May and the danger of draughts being past, the Nanninis resumed their Sunday afternoon stroll in the Borghese gardens. They were not alone, there were children bowling hoops, lovers entwined on the benches. There was a long snaking queue for ice cream. As usual they walked as far as the lake. Here on other occasions, Giulia was content to watch the sun sparkling on the water beyond the shade of the willow trees, ducks squabbling for the food thrown by children's hands and the sometimes inadequate handling of the rowing boats. But today she was resentful of the man sitting beside her and of all the habits sown over nearly thirty years of marriage. She longed for romance and adventure, for not knowing what would happen next.

1966 GIULIA

The taste of that first cigarette faded with the euphoria Giulia had felt sitting with Marco in Piazza Navona. Life resumed its usual pattern of school and home. But now that she had had a taste of freedom she was restless, finding it hard to concentrate on the chosen text for the term: Manzoni's *The Betrothed*. She spent fruitless afternoons after school, trying and failing to interpret and analyse the text. Examinations loomed but she drifted off into daydreams of Marco. Once or twice he zoomed past her on his Vespa but he didn't see her, or didn't want to.

'I don't know what's got into you,' her mother complained. 'You've changed, almost overnight. I hope you're not sickening for something.'

Just as she began to wonder what she had said or done on their cinema date that might have put him off, Marco sought her out as she sat with the dreaded Manzoni, outside the school.

'Hello Lia, where have you been hiding?'

She found herself blushing, tongue-tied, and he continued: 'I haven't seen you at *Gusto's*.'

This was the favourite café among the students, who hung around for an hour or two in the late afternoon. She wouldn't tell him that her mother always insisted she go straight home.

'No, I've been rather busy.'

'Oh I see.'

In case he'd misunderstood, she added: 'Studying, you know?' She indicated the book. 'He's very difficult.'

'Oh yes, so many adventures and plots, it's hard to keep up with them. But for some reason he's inflicted on every student.'

Giulia laughed. She felt such a relief that they had slipped back into the ease they'd had before.

Marco sat down beside her and gently closed the book. He gave her his mischievous smile. 'Does studying include Sundays? I thought perhaps you'd fancy a stroll in the Borghese Gardens.'

Sunday in her household was the day when all the family got together, when grandma and grandpapa came to lunch, but Marco had asked her to go for a walk with him.

'I'll meet you at the top of the Spanish steps,' he was saying.

How would she manage to escape the family Sunday, Giulia wondered, but she agreed. She spent the evening pondering until she came up with the perfect lie.

'Mamma, Anna Maria has had an accident and is in hospital. Her family can't visit her, this Sunday. Could I go?' Even as she spoke and her mother agreed, she was amazed at her daring. She had never done anything like this before in her life.

On Sunday morning she spent a long time going through her wardrobe, trying to decide what to wear. In the end, she chose a little shift dress with a matching jacket and low heels, considering they would be walking. She saw by the expression in Marco's eyes that she had chosen well.

They strolled along the wide avenues of trees until they reached the lake. Willows were reflected in the still water, it was a perfect summer afternoon.

'Shall we take a boat out?' Marco suggested.

"Dangerous," her mother's voice echoed in her ears. "Those boats can tip over easily and if you swallowed any of the water, you'd be very ill."

'Oh yes, that would be lovely,' she said.

He held her hand while she stepped into the boat and seated herself. He seized the oars and they glided across the lake. She felt a twinge of fear that almost immediately vanished as she watched his strong arms on the oars. She would be safe with him.

'Great, isn't it?' he laughed.

'Wonderful.' Wonderful to be free of the stifling Sunday at home, out in the fresh air. She felt she had entered the life she had dreamed about when she sat in her bedroom eyeing her reflection. The life that Lia, not Giulia, had begun. She supposed this was being in love.

Afterwards they had a drink at the café and he asked her what she would do when she left school.

'I don't know. Get a job, I suppose. I'd love to work in a dress shop.'

He smiled. 'I'll be going to university, *La Sapienza*.'

'Oh, do girls go there?'

'Some do, the ones who haven't got marriage in their immediate sights. How about you, you're not one of those, are you?'

She smiled and shook her head. I'd love to be married to you, she thought.

Later she climbed onto the Vespa and they rode through the evening traffic, zigzagging among cars, to the forbidden Via Veneto where Marco stopped to talk to a couple he knew.

'This is Lia,' He introduced her.

'How do you do, Lia,' the girl said.

Giulia sensed the girl was sizing up her relationship with Marco. She felt herself blush.

'Are you going to the Piper, this Saturday,' the girl continued, addressing Marco and ignoring her.

'I'm not sure.' His tone was offhand. 'I'll let you know.'

So this was his real life, Giulia told herself, the one her mother prevented her from joining. She felt like a child excluded from a party.

But as they said goodbye, Marco suggested a visit to Ostia Antica.

'How was your friend?' her mother asked when she arrived home.

'She'll have to be in hospital for a while.'

'Poor girl, you must visit her again.'

'I suppose I should,' she said.

******

Giulia laughed aloud at this memory of her naïve young self.

'What's so funny?' Gian Franco asked.

'Oh, nothing really.' Her gaze rested on the willow trees' reflection, bringing her back to the present.

'Shall we have some ice cream?'

'If you like.'

They sat in silence eating their ice cream, and then Gian Franco surprised her.

'I was thinking perhaps we could do a little trip.'

'What about Leonardo? We couldn't leave him on his own.'

'Only for the day, or we could go to Frascati now the evenings are getting lighter. It's a long time since we ate *porchetta*.'

XIII

'I always find it surprising that not that many people come here,' Giorgio said as they approached the Villa Giulia. 'It's a treasure trove of Etruscan art.'

Amy gazed at the impressive entrance, reminiscent of a triumphal arch. Its pale gold façade announced that a man of great wealth and taste once lived here. They stepped inside and stood in the semi-circular portico covered with frescoes. Many depicted birds: herons, swans, chickens and pigeons, species that still existed in present day Italy. Real life birds could be heard through the open windows and she wondered at how these mysterious people must have heard the same sounds all that time ago.

'The Villa was built for Pope Julius the third,' Giorgio told her. It was his favourite pleasure palace where he'd come to amuse himself with a retinue from the Vatican, no expense spared! It's a fitting place to house an Etruscan Museum because they loved banquets and parties as much as that Pope.'

There was so much to see it was bewildering. Giorgio suggested that for this visit they concentrate on the highlights. 'If we stand to read every card we'll be here forever,' he said.

They paused briefly to examine small bronze copies of the round huts these people lived in, used to contain the ashes of the dead. Cases of beautiful jewellery displayed the Etruscan love of using coloured gemstones and glass beads.

Amy's gaze was drawn to a large glass case that dominated the room. Two figures, a man and a woman reclined, their upper bodies facing front while their hips and legs seemed comfortable and relaxed, sinking into their couch. They looked young and in love, his arms around her, their feet lying together.

'It's a sarcophagus,' Giorgio's voice came to her. 'They're lying on their tomb.'

They seemed so lively, the man raising his hand with the gesture of a genial host. Their hands were empty but she wondered whether, once, they held cups of wine.

'So they're dead?' She was incredulous.

Giorgio laughed. 'It may seem strange to you but earthly pleasures were apparently a part of Etruscan mortuary rituals. If you look at the tomb paintings you'll see everything from concerts to parades, food, drink, dancing, and other mortal delights. The Etruscans, it seems, were expert revellers who wanted to take this perpetual celebration with them into the afterlife.'

She was silent, absorbing this odd combination of love and loss, death and celebration.

'Carpe diem,' Giorgio was saying. 'They seem to have been a joyous people who embraced life and physicality wholeheartedly. Who knows, perhaps they sensed they should make the very most of their days before they disappeared.'

'Disappeared?'

'Yes, Etruria was conquered by Rome in the third century BC and they left no written account of themselves.'

'How sad.'

He made to move on but Amy lingered, taking a last look at the serene couple. Were they telling her to stop this enquiry about Giorgio and simply enjoy her time with him? To celebrate the present and not pine for what had been?

As they stepped outside and the bright day met them, she felt lighthearted as if, even just for a while, she had shed her worries.

XIV

The stony face of Sister Assunta could do nothing to crush the buoyant mood of the two priests as they climbed onto the coach the following morning. Her hawkish profile as she stared resolutely through the window was inclined to reduce them to giggles. The evening before they had joined their new friends for a splendid dinner. The *maccheroncini di Campfilone*, its rich meaty sauce melting into the slender egg pasta was followed by the *brodetto* a stew packed with a countless number of shell and other fish. It was only after a decent pause, while Joan and Izzy regaled them with tales of their travels through Italy, that they were persuaded to have some ice cream.

This sumptuous feast had no effect on their delicious sleep in the hotel's comfortable beds. After breakfast they said a reluctant farewell and strolled over to the waiting coach.

The journey from Loreto passed through the Marche's lush countryside to the vine striped hills of Abruzzo.

'Pity we won't be able to visit a winery or two,' murmured Father Bruno.

'Ah yes, *Montepulciano d'Abruzzo*!' Father Eustachio's mind dwelt on the richness and complexity of that inky wine with its juicy black fruit flavours.

Little Sister Veronica's sharp ears caught this exchange. She darted a glance at the outraged figure of her superior and giggled.

Today they were bound for Manoppello, which had recently come to fame as the home of the reported Veil of The Holy Face. For centuries, few people outside the remote town had known of its existence. But recent research had revealed that the image fitted perfectly over the Turin Shroud, believed to be Jesus's burial cloth.

Nestled in a green wooded area and overlooked by the snow-covered massif of *Majella*, the Hotel *Benvenuto* awaited them. Their coach came to a halt outside and Sister Assunta, carrying a brief case, climbed out and stalked ahead of them into the reception area. Coffee and small pastries were laid out in the breakfast room. Notwithstanding the substantial breakfast they had consumed a few hours earlier, the two priests tucked in.

'They look delicious,' a voice at Father's Bruno's elbow sighed.

It was Sister Veronica, balancing a cup of coffee and a plate on which resided an almond biscuit.

'Why don't you have one?' he asked.

'We're not supposed to indulge ourselves,' the nun murmured.

They glanced over to where sister Assunta stood, deep in conversation with their guide.

'Girl of your age needs good food.' Father Bruno scooped up a cream slice and plonked it onto her plate. 'Eat it quickly before she catches you.'

Soon they were back on the coach and heading for the Sanctuary of the Holy Face, situated above the town on the slope of a wooded hill. At one point they were forced to halt for Sister Veronica who said she was feeling sick. Sister Assunta gave the priests a withering look.

'No wonder, poor young woman,' Father Bruno said. 'They probably feed her bread and water, as a rule. '

Father Eustachio nodded absently. His mind was on their forthcoming visit to see the artefact locals revered as the true face of Christ. He had read much about it, delving, as was his way, ever deeper towards his considered truth. There were several versions of the provenance of the Veil. One that it was secretly moved to Manoppello on orders from Pope Clement VII, to protect it following the Sack of Rome in 1527. According to another local tradition, an anonymous pilgrim arrived in the town in 1508 with the Veil inside a wrapped package. After handing it over, the man mysteriously disappeared.

Now he cursed himself for being so analytical. How he envied Father Bruno, who appeared to treat the saints as colleagues. He could cite a particular one for every problem under the sun. Bruno, whose feet were also planted fair and square in the physical world and could enjoy its delights without guilt. Perhaps ultimately he, Eustachio, was not cut out for the priesthood.

By now they had come to stand in the square fronting the church, to gaze on its pink and beige stone while their guide's voice droned and his thoughts continued. Did he believe in miracles? That a piece of cloth could cure leprosy? Again Father Bruno took it on face value but could he when his damned logic always got in the way? They filed into the church, a plain three-aisle interior. Ahead they saw a baroque altar and, above the tabernacle, a pillared structure containing the framed image. Having come into the presence of the mysterious piece of cloth, they stared. Even Sister Assunta was silent.

'Feel free to move around it,' the guide said. 'As you see, both sides of the cloth show a man's face.'

For a moment Eustachio couldn't make it out then, as he shifted a little, he saw the effigy of a longhaired man with broken nose, blood stained forehead and swollen cheek, his half open mouth seeming to be about to speak. Candlelight illuminated the dark bruises covering his face. His eyes gazed intensely upward so that the white of the eye could be seen under the iris, pupils wide but one larger than the other as if this man had just roused from sleep.

'Take your time,' the guide said. 'Unlike the Turin Shroud, the Veil is on show constantly, for all to see.'

Sister Assunta crossed herself and bobbed a curtsey. Sister Veronica swiftly followed suit. Still Father Eustachio pondered. Suppose none of it were true and there was no God? Where was He, after all, when that intruder sneaked into his church and defaced Saint Gertrude? Surely if He was anywhere it would be in a consecrated place? In that case, how did it place Jesus? A deluded young man… a bit of a magician to boot… who stuck out his neck and thought God would save him? If that was the truth, was there any point to life at all? Stop it Eustachio, you'll drive yourself mad with these existential questions.

'They're certain it's not just a painting?' He heard his rational voice say.

There was a shocked silence in which the older nun clucked her tongue.

'It seems not,' the guide said.

When everyone had had their fill of looking, they viewed the huge collection of votive objects left by pilgrims, elaborately framed photographs of couples or babies for whom prayers had been answered, bunches of ribbons, artificial flowers and sacred hearts. A pair of crutches was propped against a wall. Father Eustachio made the uncomfortable comparison of offerings to the gods.

'Time for lunch!' Father Bruno rubbed his hands together as they sat in the coach once more.

Father Eustachio, having experienced the dark night of the soul, found he was hoping a glass or so of *Montepulciano* might dispel his doubts.

XV

The Parco del Colle Oppio was not far from Amy's apartment. She often walked through it on her way to a little restaurant near the Colosseum. Lately, however, she had noticed more down and outs sleeping on the benches with empty beer bottles lying on the grass beside them. It was here a distressed tourist had found the latest cat victim, Concetta told her, lying near the site of archaeological ruins.

Amy reached the park as mothers were rounding up their children to take them home and before young couples arrived, so the place was fairly empty. She began to feel edgy, for Concetta as usual was late. Although she knew the homeless kept themselves to themselves, still she felt nervous and stayed on the main path. Then she saw the small figure coming towards her, still muffled in scarves although May was almost out and the evening quite warm.

They chose an area where several trees would allow them to conceal themselves. A few people passed but did not stop. An hour went by without their speaking then Concetta signalled they should move to the far entrance gate.

'It's quieter there for someone to come in unnoticed,' she whispered.

Another hour passed. Amy wondered when the park was closed. As on their previous vigil, she feared this would be futile. At that moment, Concetta grabbed her arm. 'Look!'

A tall, broad-shouldered man stood in the entrance gazing about him, his features indistinct in the failing light. He was holding a plastic bag. He started forward, glancing from left to right, seeming to peer into the shadows, scanning the area. Amy tensed, held her breath as his eyes flicked over the dappled area where they stood. She saw him stiffen as he caught sight of them, heard his muttered curse as he turned on his heel and darted back he way he had come. As he ran he dropped his scarf but didn't stop to pick it up.

'Guilty!' hissed Concetta.

'He certainly behaved very strangely,' Amy said.

'He's the murderer, I'm sure of that.'

Amy picked up the scarf and read the label.

'*Carrefour*,' she said. 'I've seen several people wearing one like this.'

"But it's another clue.'

Amy stared at the green and red striped scarf. 'It's not much of a one. They probably sell them by the dozen.'

She put her arm round the other's thin shoulders. 'I know how you feel, but we'll get him in the end. We must.'

******

For some days now there had been no further news of more cat deaths and, with Giorgio away, Amy turned her attention to the sanctuary. The arrival of warmer weather, as Susan warned, meant they should expect an increase of abandoned cats.

'Some people will think nothing of going away and leaving their cat to fend for herself on the street. You wouldn't do that to a child, would you, so why an animal?'

A concerned cat lady had brought in a tortoiseshell feline that morning. She'd found the animal crouched under a car in a busy street.

'I love torties,' Susan murmured, stroking the brindled fur. 'They're the divas of the cat world and very independent, but they can be a bit of a handful.'

Sure enough, after an hour the prettily marked cat appeared to have recovered from her recent ordeal and become quite playful.

'I'd give her a home,' Susan sighed 'But I've three already.'

They discussed a few pending adoptions awaiting home checks and examined two cats returned from surgery that were under observation. They were about to start on the afternoon's chores when Concetta arrived.

She was carrying a cardboard box, which she laid down gently on the table. Her expression was grim. 'I found this behind a dustbin near the ghetto.'

She opened the lid to reveal four small kittens within. Susan squealed, Amy gazed at the tiny creatures, trying to imagine how anyone could dump them without a thought for their survival.

'I think they're about five weeks old,' said Concetta. 'They're certainly not able to feed themselves yet. I'd rear them myself but I have two other litters at the moment.'

The kittens gazed up with their blue, slightly unfocused eyes. There were two black, a grey and one that looked as if might also be tortoiseshell. To Amy they seemed utterly helpless.

'Don't worry, we'll take them on,' said Susan.

It's a hard job. They'll need feeds day and night.' Concetta warned.

'I know, I've done it before.' She turned to Amy. 'If you can do the afternoons, I'll get Stephanie to do the mornings and I'll take over at night.'

Concetta clasped her hands. 'Susanna, you are an angel.'

After she had left, Susan showed Amy what had to be done. 'Above all, they need to be kept warm. Kittens can't regulate their own body temperature, they usually rely on the heat of their mother. As they probably haven't had their mother's milk, their immune systems are weak and they could easily die.'

The process of sterilising equipment and preparing was quite lengthy and Amy felt daunted until she sat down to give the kittens a first feed from a nursing bottle. To her delight, three of them had a strong suck and drank eagerly from the bottle of special formula. It was the fourth that was struggling so she switched to using a syringe.

'Be careful,' Susan warned. 'Just drip small quantities onto his tongue. You can massage the throat to encourage him to swallow.'

Her whole being seemed to be concentrated on this small creature, willing it to take sustenance. Eventually she laid him down among his squirming siblings, but still couldn't tear herself away. Time passed and she realised Susan was preparing to shut the office.

'I don't want to leave him,' she said. 'He's taken so little milk.'

'Don't worry, I'll take over,' Susan said. 'I'll sleep here tonight.' She indicated the sofa bed in the corner of the office.

Amy made a quick decision. 'I won't open the spice stall tomorrow. I'll be here all day. I want to take care of that weak one.'

Susan frowned. 'Amy, they don't all pull through, you know. We'll do our best but...'

Amy spent a restless night, getting up in the early hours to sit by the window and gaze down on the practically deserted street. A solitary wanderer was caught momentarily in the light of a street lamp, and then disappeared into the gloom. She wondered how her tiny kitten was faring, prayed he would get through the night. Then, as it often happened when she was feeling particularly alone, an image of Davide came into her mind. She remembered the day they had gone to the garden of the monsters near Viterbo, a strange and melancholy place filled with grotesque creatures, hewn from volcanic rock. He had led her among three-headed dogs, a being half-female half-serpent, a proudly prancing Pegasus. She saw violence in the roughly sculpted giant tearing an equally huge opponent to pieces, a snarling dragon in the death-grip of two lions, a troll with a huge gaping mouth and the inscription: *All reason departs*. The enigmatic sculptures and inscriptions had compounded her sense of the mystery that surrounded Davide. Soon after that he was gone with no firm promise they would meet again, only asking her to remember his name.

'Oh Davide, why?' she whispered and experienced the sense of futility, which comes sometimes when the body is at its lowest ebb. 'How could I ever forget?'

Back at the sanctuary, Susan greeted her, looking remarkably bright after her disturbed night. The runt kitten was much less lively than the others but he was still alive. Amy took the tiny bundle onto her knee, laying him on the blanket-covered warm pad. There was a moment when he opened his eyes and his milky gaze seemed to regard her. 'Oh my darling,' she whispered. But then they closed again. All morning she sat there, sometimes cuddling him against her, cosily wrapped up. She found herself praying 'please don't let him die'. At noon she fed the other kittens and tried to syringe a little formula into the weak one's mouth. There was a tiny mew of protest and he turned his head away. Her mind was now fixed on the little form, willing him to fight. Tears ran down her face. Then Stephanie was beside her. She hadn't realised the Australian had taken Susan's place.

'Let me take him.'

Amy shook her head.

'Just for a moment.'

She allowed the other to lift the now limp creature to the light. There was a moment's silence. 'I'm afraid he's gone,' Stephanie said in an uncharacteristically gentle voice.

Amy felt her stomach lurch. It couldn't be true. In a few hours, her attachment to this tiny creature had grown incredibly strong. She let her arms fall uselessly to the sides of her chair, bent her head and wept.

******

'How can they?' she asked Susan later. 'First this cat poisoner and now these monsters abandoning tiny kittens.'

The American had returned to find Amy huddled in a corner of the office with the dead kitten in her arms. Gently she had taken it away and laid it in a shoebox, to be buried in her garden.

'What kind of person could do this? I don't understand.'

'There are some ignorant people out there, Amy. They won't have their animals neutered for several reasons. One is religion, we are living in a predominately Roman Catholic country, but another is just not thinking animals warrant spending money on. Do you know, I've been accused of being a cat murderer because I've urged neutering?'

Amy had made up her mind. She remembered Salvatore had a relative who was a journalist. She would ask him to put them in touch when she saw him at the market in the morning.

XVI

'I hope your papa won't forget we have an appointment with the vet, this afternoon,' Giulia told the hunched back of Leonardo. 'The moment he gets chatting to that friend of his, he loses all track of time.'

After the trip to Georgia, which, she suspected, had not fulfilled Gian Franco's dreams, she had hoped the friendship with Antonio would falter, but apparently it had gathered strength. The pair seemed able to carry on long conversations in a bar, every time they met.

All was ready and waiting: an early lunch, the pasta sauce gently bubbling. Leonardo's carrier sat on the bed with the door closed so he wouldn't see it until the last moment. She'd ordered a taxi. Now she waited anxiously to eat and be gone.

For the past week she had been worried about the ginger cat. As a rule he was a constant if picky eater of the choice morsels of fish or meat she offered. Lately, he had often sniffed at them and turned away. Granted he still took up his surveillance of the city from his windowsill perch, but now he would quickly grow bored and slink down to the sofa where he curled up and slept. What was wrong with him?

Half-heartedly she watched the colonel reading the weather forecast. He looked as spruce as ever but her mind was distracted, wondering what the consultation with *Dottore* Turiano might reveal. She jumped when she heard Gian Franco's key in the door.

Her husband looked subdued. He told her that Antonio and a group of similarly bachelor-placed friends were planning an autumn trip to Acqualagna for the truffle fair. They ate the Pasta Norma in silence, which Giulia broke by asking why he didn't go with them.

Gian Franco shrugged: 'when we don't know how ill Leonardo might be? I wouldn't want to leave you to deal with it alone.'

Giulia laid down her fork. 'Don't talk like that.'

'We have to face facts.'

She stared at him. 'What do you mean?'

'He's nearly eight. Cats don't live forever.'

'Nonsense. That's no age. He's just gone off his food for a bit.'

What was in her husband's mind? Did he still harbour the feeling that Leonardo was more important to her than he? For the past months she had tried to make amends for considering him second best to her youthful dreams. She had come to terms with her life as it was now, hadn't she? She eyed the remaining pasta on her plate and picked up her fork. Her mother, who had lived through the war years when the country practically starved, had taught her not to waste good food.

The practice was busy when they arrived with Leonardo who was unperturbed by his taxi ride. He remained silent as they sat in the waiting room while around them other cats complained loudly. Was this a good sign? Giulia wondered.

Dottore Turiano, a man who treated all his clients like children, did nothing to dispel her anxiety. She watched as his practised fingers palpated Leonardo's body then put him on the scales. There was a pause.

'Has he lost weight?' she asked.

The vet grunted. 'A little, though he's still heavier than I'd like him to be.'

He opened Leonardo's mouth and examined his teeth. He sounded his heart and fetched some clippers to cut his claws. 'He's in good health,' he pronounced. 'Physically that is. Psychologically, I'd say he's lonely.'

'But he's hardly ever left alone,' Gian Franco said. 'There's usually one of us at home, if not both.'

'Look at it this way,' said *Dottore* Turiano. 'He's an indoor cat and he doesn't have the social interaction of one that roams and encounters other cats. Perhaps that is what he has started to miss.' He glanced at his watch. 'I'll just give him a vitamin injection, then it's up to you.'

Having settled a substantial bill, the Nanninis stood outside the clinic waiting for a taxi.

'So where do we go from here?' queried Gian Franco. 'Another cat?'

'I don't know. Let's ask Amy.'

The following morning, Gian Franco turned up at the spice stall, which Amy had recovered herself enough to reopen. He accepted the morning's taster offering of spicy minestrone with garlic croutons before relating the visit to the vet.

'Maybe a companion would be something you could try,' Amy suggested. 'But be careful how you introduce it. Cats can be social but they're also territorial. We don't like it if somebody comes into our house and takes over. It's the same with cats. I won't be at the sanctuary for a few days but Stephanie can sort you out.'

It was a difficult choice and Giulia and Gian Franco took over an hour to decide. Male or female? Young or older? Then there was the decision to make over colour for Stephanie had produced several: A tabby, black, tortoiseshell, ginger. Wouldn't another ginger cat offend Leonardo?

'It's the temperament match you should consider,' the Australian suggested. 'What kind of a cat is Leonardo?'

'Quiet, I suppose you'd say, wouldn't you, Gian Franco?'

He nodded.

Perhaps you want a cat that will encourage him to play? It excludes this little chap and maybe this one.'

They were left with a choice between two and decided on the tortoiseshell. As she knew Giulia's background, Stephanie allowed them to take Macchiato without a home visit.

'I just hope we're doing the right thing,' Giulia remarked as they rode home in a taxi.

XVII

GIULIA 1966

The visit to Ostia Antica seemed to consolidate their relationship. They had wandered among the ruins of warehouses, apartments and shopping arcades conjuring images of how these ancient Romans lived. As they reached the tavern with its small sink and shelves that once displayed food and drinks for sale, Marco took her hand.

'It doesn't matter how many times I come here, I always have the strange feeling that I'll see a toga just vanishing round a corner or hear a shop keeper calling his wares. The atmosphere is extraordinary.'

Aware of his nearness, the scent of his musky cologne, Giulia felt a surge of joy. During the time she had known him, she had always feared each outing would be the last. Now there was an easiness between them and they seemed to have passed that uncertain phase.

'Were they really like us?' she asked. All that time ago?'

Marco laughed. 'What do you think, they had two noses or something? You are a funny little thing.'

She bit her lip, ashamed. 'Sorry, that was stupid of me.'

'Not at all, I mean you're sweet.' He kissed her on the cheek and her heart leapt.

Later as they sat on a bench eating the picnic Marco had brought, he said: 'Mamma would like to meet you,' He didn't look too happy about it. 'She asked me who I was taking to Ostia Antica and I had to tell her.'

Giulia thought of her continuing subterfuge, her mother's belief in the fictitious sick friend, the hospital visits. 'You didn't have to tell her, if you didn't want to.'

He laughed. 'You don't know my mother.'

What did he mean by that? She began to feel alarmed. 'But I'm sure she'll like you,' Marco added.

Giulia decided it was time to confess to her own mother, but the very idea of it made her mouth dry and she kept on putting it off. The days passed and she'd made a few half-hearted attempts and then finally blurted it out as she was helping with the dishes. She was taken aback by her mother's reaction.

'Oh darling, they're such a good family. I can't wait to tell everybody. Imagine having a Giordano as a son in law!'

Giulia panicked. 'Mamma, I'm only going for coffee.'

'Ah but it's a step in the right direction. I understand how these things work. Now let's think what you'll wear.'

At this Giulia rebelled. If she let her mother have her way, she'd be dressed as if she were going to a cocktail party. Marco's style was smart, admittedly, but deceptively so, and she would follow suit.

'I've decided already,' her tone was calm. 'I shall wear that pink dress with the white collar and cuffs.

'But you've worn it so many times before.'

'I know, because I feel comfortable in it.'

Her mother sighed. 'That's hardly the point.'

Nevertheless, when the day dawned Giulia felt nervous, she was so anxious to make a good impression. As they rode the Vespa uphill towards the palatial building of Monte Verde, she was glad she'd let her hair hang loose rather than pinned up into an elaborate style as her mother had suggested. It would surely have come undone and look awful. In the reception area they were confronted by a snooty porter demanding to know the names of *Signora* Giordano's visitors even though, as Marco told him, 'you know exactly who I am'. Only then would the man deign to lift the telephone.

'Your son is here, *signora*,' he announced. 'Do you wish me to send him up?' Eyeing Giulia, he added: 'He has a young lady with him, a *Signorina* Altavilla.'

'Send them up, Horatio.' Giulia heard a woman's voice.

They rode up in a velvet-lined lift hung with speckled mirrors before stepping out into a spacious, high-ceilinged marble foyer. A door opened and a tiny woman stood there. She wore a necklace of rather large pearls at the throat of her cream two-piece and her dark hair was perfectly styled.

'Marco!' she cried, holding out her arms in a dramatic gesture. He moved forward to embrace her. Over his shoulder, her bright, dark eyes surveyed Giulia.

He drew away. 'Mamma, this is Lia.'

'So you are the *signorina* I've heard so much about.'

What had Marco told her?

'But what a pretty dress you're wearing,' *Signora* Giordano exclaimed. 'It makes you look like a little girl.'

Giulia immediately wondered if her mother had been right to suggest she dressed more formally. She detected a disparaging note in the woman's voice.

She led the way into the *salone*, which Giulia noted was a grander version of theirs at home: the same ornate, dark furniture, though this must be the genuine article. A tray set with coffee cups and a silver cake stand stacked with pastries stood on a polished table with curved legs. An anxious-looking woman in a flowered overall carried in a silver coffee pot.

'Thank you, Serafina,' *Signora* Giordano waved a manicured hand. The woman nodded and silently went.

'So, dear, tell me about yourself,' she began.

Giulia, who had just taken a cream filled pastry, set it down. It had been a mistake anyway. How was she going to eat it without the contents squishing all over the place?

'I live with my mother and father in Trastevere and I go to the same college as Marco.'

'And what does your father do?'

'He's a civil servant, *signora*.'

'I see. In what department?'

'The Revenue Office,'

'Ah! A tax collector.' There was a pause. 'And your mother?'

'My mother?'

'Yes, what does she do?"

'Oh… she's… just a housewife.'

'Just? Oh my dear Lia, that is one of the most important things a woman can do: to keep a house and take care of her children.'

Giulia considered this. 'Well, there's only me.'

'And do you help your Mamma?'

'Yes.'

'With the cooking and housework?'

Giulia paused. Her mother ruled the kitchen and allowed no one to come near even a saucepan, but what was the required answer?

'Oh yes,' she said.

Signora Giordano appeared satisfied with her answers.

She signalled to Serafina who slid into the room with fresh coffee. Gently but firmly she removed Giulia's plate with the uneaten pastry. As silently as before, she left the room.

Signora Giordano took up the silver coffee pot. 'I have to tell you that my son is a very special young man with a bright future ahead of him. It is important he makes the right choices in his relationships.' She paused to offer the plate of pastries and Giulia took a small plain looking cake. 'You seem a well brought up young lady.'

Marco murmured: 'Mamma!'

'No Marco, let me have my say. We have had disappointments in this family you see, Lia. My other son... well Paolo... has rather let us down.'

'Mamma! I'm sure Lia doesn't want to hear all this.'

His mother ignored him. 'Of course you must forgive me, my dear. A mother only wants the best for her children, as I know one day you will discover.'

Giulia was beginning to feel at a loss and, searching for something to say that would change the subject, directed attention to a rather dark picture hanging on the wall. 'Who is the gentleman?' she asked.

'That is my husband, my Osvaldo. He was such a wonderful man, you see, perfect in every way, taken from me far too young and never an angry word between us.' She wiped her eyes on a lace handkerchief.

Marco murmured: 'Mamma, don't upset yourself. '

'I'm fine, *figlio mio*, it is just the thought of him, it makes me emotional.'

Giulia found this outburst embarrassing. She stared fixedly at the portrait. What kind of a life had this woman led poor Osvaldo, she wondered, to dispatch him so early.

Meanwhile *Signora* Giordano continued: 'All I ask the Lord is to give me grandchildren and allow me some joy in my old age.'

'Si, Mamma, si.'

It was obvious Marco had heard this story many times and Giulia was amazed at his patience.

'Have you lost anyone close to you?' She had turned her attention to Giulia.

'My grandmother.'

'Then you will understand pain, the longing to hear a dear voice again.'

Gloom seemed to have descended on the room and conversation struggled on until release came with the tinny sound of the ormolu clock striking five. As if this were a secret sign, *Signora* Giordano got to her feet.

'It has been a pleasure to meet you, Lia, I hope you will visit again.' She held out her hand. It felt like a bird's claw.

'I'll see you tomorrow, Mamma,' Marco lingered to say as he embraced her.

Giulia was already at the door, held open for them by Serafina, who had soundlessly appeared. She was longing for some fresh air. They made their way to where the Vespa was parked under a tree.

'Mamma seemed to like you,' Marco said. 'But I'm sorry she went on about grandchildren. She can't wait to get me married.' He smiled at her. 'Thank heavens you're not one of those girls who spend their time mooning over rings and wedding dresses.'

Giulia laughed and shook her head. She climbed onto the Vespa behind him and they set off. Her mind was elsewhere as she wondered whether she was more her mother's daughter than she cared to admit. If Marco didn't see her as a future wife, then where was she?

XVIII

When she could stir herself to get out of bed at dawn, Amy's favourite Sunday morning destination was a particular corner of Trastevere where, for a few hours, the area was transformed into the crazily busy Porta Portese market. She revelled in the lively atmosphere, the air filled with the sound of cheerful calls and banter from the traders, the sense of being part of the 'real' Rome. Endless stalls offered hours of browsing, an invitation to rummage through junk and treasures and discover a vintage item. She'd learned to walk past the plastic and imported goods, her eye attuned to picking out a piece of jewellery crafted many years ago, or examining the expert stitching on a leather bag or belt. Whether she unearthed a hidden gem or not, there was something quintessentially Italian about the whole experience. Today as always, she began at the stall set up near a former bank where the trader dumped a medley of objects on two, rickety trestle tables. She ignored the carved wooden chess set, some tattered books and an effigy of Donald Duck made in obviously imitation bronze. She knew there would be more interesting objects to find.

Over time she had built up a connection with the elderly trader, stopping to engage in conversation rather than bark questions at him, as many did. She would launch the exchange by showing enthusiasm for his wares, sharing with him his passion and thus developed his trust. Instead of turning away with an 'I'll think about it,' she'd come right out with 'I'm afraid the price is a bit more than I can afford to pay at the moment.' This might lead to the question of how much she'd like to pay and from there they would embark on haggling. To her surprise, for it had seemed unfamiliar at first, Amy discovered she could do this rather well. The secret, she'd learned, was not to allow the trader to think she was weakening, to hold fast, until it was he with a shrug of his shoulders, a '*va bene*' delivered her prize. This way she'd secured more than one genuine bargain. These days, she understood his tactic of which new comers were unaware. For clients he knew, the unmentioned price was always 2,000 lira. It didn't matter what it was, he would charge them 2,000 lira. For those who were not regular shoppers the object in question reverted to 'special price'.

After Amy had secured the vintage pendant with its inlaid butterfly motif that she planned to send as the 'something old' item for her cousin's wedding, she commented on the weather.

'Ah the weather!' The trader wiped imaginary sweat from his brow. 'So much rain in April, too much rain and now… what do you think? Will the summer continue so hot? My God it beats down on one, even with this umbrella over my stall. *Signorina*, I suffer, believe me I suffer. I should have been born in your country.'

She started to commiserate when something caught her eye. Not something, someone. She froze, the trader's voice fading as all her attention focussed on the man who stood a few stalls away. He was tall and broad shouldered, he wore a white tee shirt and as he moved away she saw his jeans were orange. She could not see his face but something about the back of his head, his easy gait, made her think it was Giorgio. Giorgio! But how could it be? He was on the dig at Tarquinia, or so he'd told her. Excusing herself she pushed her way through the throng of people in the direction he'd taken, but he moved too fast and was absorbed by the crowd. Amy halted, her heart beating fast. She needed to escape the market, which, a few moments ago, had seemed good hearted and fun. She found a table in a kerbside café and sank down, her body sticky with sweat. She gazed at the newspaper wrapped package she had grabbed from the trader. Her hands were trembling as she stowed it in her bag. Her mind was in turmoil: if it were Giorgio, what was he doing here at the market? He'd always laughed at her pride in finding a bargain, warning her, too, of pickpockets. Had he lied to her because he was tired of her company? She was so deep in thought that when the waiter came for her order she looked up at him with startled eyes.

'Okay?' his tone was concerned.

She forced a laugh and ordered a Cinzano. Her watch told her it was almost time for lunch. Later, as she always did, she stopped at a nearby pizzeria to buy a slice to take away, but kept her eye on the crowds searching for a pair of orange jeans.

IXX

Salvatore's call was answered by his cousin, the journalist who, a year ago, had given Amy such a good write up of her spice stall. She was a woman of about Amy's age, small and plump, whose dark rimmed glasses gave her a studious look. Rosina took her job very seriously and her first question was to ask if Amy really wanted to be so unequivocal.

'I can guarantee you'll make some enemies,' she said.

At her request they had met at the cat sanctuary, although Amy would have preferred it to be elsewhere. She was still grieving the death of the kitten. Rosina toured the various rooms taking photographs and was enchanted when Shadow graced her with his presence.

'What a beautiful cat!'

'Isn't he?' Amy said with the pride of ownership.

'I'd love to scoop him up and take him home with me,' said Rosina.

'I'm afraid he's not up for adoption. He's our mascot cat,' Amy lied. She couldn't bear the idea of giving him up.

'Don't worry, I was only joking. My job takes me out so much, it wouldn't be right for me to have a pet.'

Rosina opened her notebook. 'Shall we sit over there and begin?'

Amy needed no encouragement. It was a relief to unburden herself to someone and to feel that at last she was doing something constructive about the situation. She spoke of the recent spate of cat poisoning, which had started up again in Rome. She described the agonising death these animals suffered and saw Rosina recoil. Before she could stop herself she was also telling her about the dumped kittens they'd found.

'They put them in the rubbish, they tie them up in a bag and throw them into the sea, they...'

'Please!' Rosina covered her ears. 'I think I've got the picture.'

'Did you know a cat can have three litters a year and there can be at least four kittens in each? Multiple that by twelve to fourteen years and you'll see the potential overpopulation. The solution is easy: neuter them.'

Rosina stopped writing. 'So?'

'Too many people are ignorant, apathetic and, of course, misguided in their religious beliefs.' She ran her hand over Shadow's back. 'Roman Catholicism has a lot to answer for.' The truth has to be told, she thought.

As the journalist closed her notebook she asked again: 'are you sure you want me to print all this? It could be quite inflammatory.'

An image of the tortoiseshell kitten came into her mind, the moment when its tiny body went limp.

'Yes, I'm quite sure. Why not?' Amy said.

The article came out the following week and Concetta arrived at the sanctuary bearing a bouquet of roses.

She embraced Amy. 'Well done, my dear! She's such a good, brave girl, isn't she?' she appealed to Susan.

'Brave or foolhardy,' the American remarked. 'I just hope there aren't any repercussions.'

"Nonsense! These things must be said. Otherwise will anything change?'

******

Giorgio called her to say he was back in town. Amy's spirits rose and she realised she had missed him. They met the following evening and went to eat at the unpretentious pizzeria near the Trevi Fountain. He looked tired and she asked him if he'd been overworking.

'The problem we are fighting is the *tombaroli*, the tomb robbers. As I told you before, there is a huge illicit trade in these priceless artefacts. I've stayed up several nights at the site of the dig. But the situation is more complex than that. There are Italians who question why all finds automatically belong to the State. They see no reason why finders shouldn't be keepers.' He laughed. 'An uncle of mine was so indignant when I accused him of being a tomb robber. "I'm a collector" he said, "I would never sell them."'

Amy smiled absentmindedly. Into her mind came the image of the tall, well-built man she'd glimpsed at the flea market. The man who had run away and dropped his scarf in the park had been tall and well built, too. But how could it have been Giorgio if he was miles away? She longed to dispel these doubts but something held her back from questioning him. Instead she asked: 'Where is the dig exactly?'

'I thought I'd told you, it's at Tarquinia.'

Tarquinia was only a short distance from Rome, near enough to make it back and forth in a few hours. It could have been him she saw and yet... his nice, open face was full of anxiety for the precious artefacts. She put the thought aside, reached out for the carafe and refilled his glass.

'Well relax now. You deserve it.'

He smiled. 'I'd say you're sweet but...'

'But?'

'Amy, did you really think it wise to give that interview?'

He'd read the article then. 'Not you too?'

'So I'm not alone in thinking you were courting trouble?'

Amy had taken up her fork. She laid it down again. 'Please Giorgio don't criticise me, it's something I had to do. I'm concerned about the way these cats are treated. Let's not waste time arguing about it.'

'OK.' He turned his attention to his pizza, cutting it into neat strips, and the awkward moment passed.

Afterwards they strolled through the historic centre and Giorgio took her arm. The May evening was balmy and the streets were full of couples and families enjoying the Roman spring. Amy had the now familiar feeling that this city was where she belonged. The Colosseum, the illuminated Forum and Piazza Venezia were like old friends. They walked on and came to Piazza Navona where they bought ice creams and sat on a bench to eat them. For once she didn't compare Giorgio's casual behaviour with Davide, who would have suggested a seat on a café terrace.

'I was thinking of going down to Reggio Calabria to see the Riace Warrior Bronzes,' he said.

'Oh?'

'Maybe you haven't heard of them? They're a pair of Greek statues, probably sculpted in the fifth century. In 1972, a man was snorkelling when he saw an arm protruding from the ocean bed. Considering the area, he thought it was a Mafia victim, at first, but then these wonderful figures were dredged up and identified. I've been promising myself I'd go and see them for ages.'

Amy had been gazing at the magnificent figures of the Bernini fountain, marvelling at the play of muscle and sinew, born of stone, and then her attention was averted. A street performer dressed in a cowboy costume and coated in silver paint, posed at the base of the fountain.

Here he stood motionless, only raising an arm in salute when someone dropped a coin into the box at his feet. Now that she'd noticed him, she realised there were other motionless figures dotted around the square.

She wondered where the idea came from? Wasn't it a rather cheeky notion to occupy what had been the great sculptor's space for centuries? Or was it rooted in the living statues of characters like Pygmalion, the statue who came to life? Whatever the origin, she found him as mesmerising as the work of the great sculptor.

She became aware Giorgio had stopped speaking and was looking at her enquiringly. 'Would you?' he said. 'Like to come with me?'

Amy stared at him in surprise. What was he suggesting: a romantic excursion or simply a friendly gesture? She looked back to the cowboy, remembering Paolo's ambiguous remarks about the Bevacqua family. Was she prepared to embark on yet another mystery after that of Davide?

Giorgio seemed to sense her hesitation. 'Think about it,' he said. 'It wouldn't be for another week or so. I have to go back to Tarquinia for another few days.'

XX

Much later, Amy sat at the window of the apartment. Behind her the lamp light cast mysterious shadows over the room. As they often did, her thoughts turned to those dreary months after Davide had gone. So brief was their time together and yet he stayed in her mind like a persistent note of music or a perfume. As Paolo had said, he knew being sensible was not easy in affairs of the heart, but he wouldn't want her to become like Marco.

Every time they'd met, she'd felt this sense of some mystery that came between them. She remembered the ending of their day in Bracciano when they walked along the lakeside path and sat there until the sun began to set. The sky had flamed above the water and tinged it scarlet. They stayed in silence with Davide's arm round her shoulders and then she turned to him to say how beautiful it was and found him gazing at her. He pulled her to him and she gave herself up to the kiss, wanting it to go on and on. But all too soon the hoot of horns and Rome's evening crowds had taken over from the tranquillity of the lake.

As they parked outside the apartment, her curiosity had got the better of her: 'What is it you do exactly?'

He turned his head away. 'Don't ask me, Amy, please.'

There'd been a note of desperation in his voice, which made her put out her hand to touch his arm.

'You can tell me,'

He shook his head, then to her surprise laid his head on her shoulder and sighed. 'Oh, *cara* Amy, what am I to do now that I've met you?'

His life in Naples remained an enigma. Now she was facing yet another puzzle with Giorgio who on the surface had seemed uncomplicated, until she'd had these mysterious sightings. The invitation to see the bronze statues was enticing but did she really want to get further involved if it ended in heartbreak? If only she had someone she could talk to. Maybe Susan?

The American woman's expression was serious when she arrived at the sanctuary the following afternoon. A couple had come into the office and handed her a note. 'I'm sorry, I read it but it's for you.'

Written in Italian, it was brief but to the point. This is to warn you to keep your nose out of things that don't concern you, foreigner.

Amy murmured, 'Stupid, ignorant people,' but found she was shaking.

'I did warn you publishing that article could bring trouble.'

Amy was unrepentant, recalling the tiny kittens that were thrown away like rubbish.

'I know how strongly you feel. But I've lived here longer than you, sweetie,' Susan said. 'I've learned there are times when you keep your mouth shut.'

'And cats will go on being poisoned by people like these?' For the first time she was angry with Susan. 'At least Concetta is on my side.' She screwed the note up and tossed it into the wastepaper basket.

'Believe me, I understand,' the other tried.

'Do you? Amy eyed the little figure in the flowered apron. 'Do you really? I wonder. Perhaps you've been here so long you've lost any empathy for the poor creatures.'

She went to find Shadow who, as he often did, came to her at times when she needed him. She stroked his silky grey fur and meeting his amber gaze, she was overwhelmed with a longing to protect him, protect all these creatures she'd discovered such an affinity with. She murmured: 'If anyone harmed you I'd kill them.'

When her afternoon shift was over, she left without saying goodbye to Susan. She found herself turning in the direction of the church of St Gertrude of Nivells. She loved this outwardly unprepossessing church for the calm simplicity of its interior. Here, believer or not, one could find peace.

At that moment someone spoke. 'Good afternoon, *signorina*.'

Father Eustachio appeared even leaner than before, his cassock hanging in folds about him and his face seemed to have acquired new wrinkles.

'Good afternoon, Father. Do you remember me?'

'Of course, you are Amy, the little *gattara* from Largo Argentina. Can I help you?'

What a memory the man had. Her last visit must have been months ago.

'I'm very anxious,' she found herself telling him. 'There is someone out there killing cats. He nodded and to her surprise said: 'I am, too. There is evil abroad. The statue of St Gertrude has also been vandalised.'

They walked through the shadowy church, empty except for an old woman knelt in prayer. They halted by an alcove, lit by a row of flickering candles.

'Here she is, restored by an excellent cleaner, thank the Lord. She was covered in red paint.'

Amy stared at the figure of the young woman, her head covered by a wimple and veil from which a length of braided hair escaped. Her lips parted in a smile that showed her teeth. She cradled a large cat and as before, their two pairs of eyes seemed to be gazing directly at her.

'I've come to feel quite protective of her,' said the priest, 'which is surprising when you consider I am not an animal lover, particularly of cats. However, I like the inscription.' He read it aloud: 'I will not leave you comfortless.'

Amy put some lire into the little box and lit a candle. She was drawn back to the arresting gaze of the saint and her cat, and felt an overwhelming sense of consolation.

XXI

Alone, after the elderly woman had followed Amy out of the church, Father Eustachio advanced towards the crucified Christ above the altar. 'Show yourself, Lord,' he whispered. 'Let me once again see your face.'

Since the trip to view the sacred Face in Monnoppolo and in spite of his struggles, his doubt had grown and become a raw grief that woke him in the night to a terrible darkness within him, as if everything was dead. He waited. The silence in the church seemed to intensify itself into a tangible absence. God appeared to have deserted him. His knuckles gripping the altar rails shone white as he knelt and bowed his head, not wanting to look at the hanging figure anymore. If there was no God then there could be no soul, if there was no soul then Jesus was not true. He wept.

It was here that Father Bruno discovered him. Arriving at his friend's house and finding he was not at home, he had been directed by the housekeeper to the church. Father Eustachio was alerted of his presence by the light touch on his shoulder. He scrambled to his feet and smoothed his cassock.

'What are you doing here?'

Startled by his brusque tone Father Bruno replied: 'I was invited for supper, don't you remember?'

'Of course, I'm sorry. It went out of my head.'

'Not a problem, but I am concerned about you. Tell me what is going on, old chap.'

Father Eustachio made a attempt to pass it off but his friend was having none of it. 'Come on, let's go over to your study and you can tell me. Perhaps,' his tone was sly, 'a glass of wine would help.'

******

When he saw there was no use trying to foil his fellow priest, Father Eustachio decided to come straight to the point. 'The truth is this: I think I may have to leave the church. I'm no longer worthy of being a priest.'

A shocked silence followed this bombshell.

'I've lost my faith, you see, Bruno. I long for God but feel rejected. My world feels empty with no faith or wish to save souls. Heaven means nothing.'

Father Bruno took a gulp of wine and considered this. 'How long have you been feeling these doubts?'

'I think it was since our trip to Mannoppolo, but it may have been coming on before that. When we saw that piece of cloth, something told me it was a fake.'

'Who can know, but many believe it to be true.'

'But they don't know for sure. There is no evidence.'

'That's faith for you, one must believe in spite of there being no evidence, and it's normal to struggle and doubt. It's all part of the faith journey. God's not keen on the self-righteous, He wants us to wrestle with Him. He wants anything but unthinking faith.'

This was a new side to the usually jovial Bruno and Father Eustachio looked at him in surprise. 'Have you had doubts then?' he asked.

'Once or twice, I think we all do at times when a child dies or someone who's never done any harm gets ill. Mother Teresa saw more than her fair share of that and she recorded the grave doubts she had. She made her doubt work for her, integrated it into her faith, and her uncertainty about God and the future deepened that faith over time. This has always encouraged me that I am not alone.' He smiled. 'And now after all that, my throat is feeling a little dry.'

Father Eustachio took up the bottle. Bruno's words had had a powerful effect. He felt overwhelmed by them. Was it true that, however much he'd wrestled and kicked at God, he was unconditionally loved? At the same time it dawned on him that he would probably always fight with his questioning self. But there came a certain sense of relief that he was no longer running away but might return to one who knew his struggles were all part of his soul's growth.

'You're a good man, Bruno,' he said.

Bruno raised his glass. 'More like God's jester, I'd say!'

XXII

Gian Franco folded the newspaper with a sigh. 'Our friend Amy is inclined to be rather extreme, I'm afraid.'

'Nonsense.' Giulia had already read the article. 'Situations like these demand extreme measures. I made that *denuncia* over two weeks ago and there's been absolutely no news from the police. I expect it's just been filed away.'

She ran a duster over the spotless coffee table and folded it away. 'I'll be off out now. Keep an eye on those two cats while I'm away. I've put Macchiato in the bathroom just to be on the safe side.'

Introducing the feisty tortoiseshell was proving an uphill job.

Gian Franco's gaze had strayed to the television. With Giulia out of the way, he could have some uninterrupted viewing of Rete 4 and, with any luck, the curvaceous Selina.

******

Giulia and Amy left behind the roar of traffic speeding along Viale Ostiense, to enter the Protestant Cemetery, a peaceful and romantic space. In single file, they followed the narrow pathways edged with neat hedges that ran between the rows of tombstones and monuments. There were pomegranate trees and tiny purple flowers. A black cat lay in the shade of towering cypress trees. Neither spoke as they left the shadowed paths and entered a more open, green space, pausing for a moment by two simple gravestones standing side by side: John Keats and his friend, Joseph Severn. They moved on to Marco's tombstone. It was a simple one with an engraving of an open book and its inscription: *A heart breaking can be as quiet as a feather falling. No one hears it but you.*

Giulia laid her monthly offering, on this occasion a posy of spring flowers.

They stood together in the tranquil cemetery, oblivious of the footsteps and voices of other visitors, the sun warm on their backs.

Amy broke the silence. 'Do you think it was true, that he died of a broken heart?'

'He was a romantic and guided by his feelings rather than practical considerations. The Giordano family had always married for logical, pragmatic reasons where both sets of parents held the same version of how a relationship should work.'

Amy thought of her cousin's imminent wedding. 'It sounds very much how my mother sees things.'

'Whereas you?'

'I suppose I'm a romantic too. When I met Davide I was drawn to him in spite of any misgivings and I knew it was right. The fact we come from such different backgrounds didn't seem to matter.'

They gazed in silence at the gravestone. The peace was awe-inspiring, broken only by the twittering of swallows. The warmth of the sun increased.

Giulia laid a hand on her arm. 'Poor Amy, it's hard for you. But don't be like Marco. Don't waste your life being unhappy. You must move on.'

Amy seized the opportunity to broach the subject of Giorgio's invitation to Calabria, and her hesitation to accept. Without mentioning the odd sightings she'd had of him, she told Giulia of her doubts about being further involved with another man.

'Paolo has hinted he comes from a strange family,' she said. 'But he shies away when I ask him to explain.'

Giulia laughed. 'That sounds like Paolo. He'll never commit himself to actually criticising someone.'

They turned away from the tragic words on the gravestone and strolled between the low box hedges and out of the cemetery gates. As usual they went to a nearby café for their espresso.

'I had doubts about Gian Franco to begin with,' Giulia began. 'We met at the library where he worked, he invited me for coffee and we became friends. My mother was bitterly disappointed when I told her that Marco wasn't interested in marriage. She was convinced he would change his mind and that I should hang around, wait until he proposed, but he'd made it very clear. She tried to take over my life again but I wasn't having any of it. If I'd learned anything from being with Marco, it was to be my own person. I even smoked.'

Amy laughed. 'I bet not as much as my mother!'

'Yes, that was one of the things Maria Giordano disliked about her. She said she could smell the smoke on your mother's hair.'

Amy brought the subject back to her quandary. 'Are you saying I should stop thinking about Davide?'

Giulia sighed. 'I can't tell you to do that but maybe you should give Giorgio a chance. It's not as if you're marrying the man are you? A little trip together might settle your mind.'

In the silence that followed Amy decided. 'Thank you, Giulia, you're a good friend.'

Giulia patted her arm. You're a lovely woman.'

They were enjoying each other's company and wanted to prolong the time together. The waiter brought more coffees.

'How are you getting on with the new cat?' Amy wanted to know.

'Ah that's another story!'

******

When Gain Franco and Giulia chose a tortoiseshell cat they had no notion of the term tortitude. After the two cats had been tentatively introduced, Leonardo had decided to have nothing to do with Macchiato, while she seemed hell bent on attracting his attention. A pretty young cat, she appeared to have a split personality, one moment purring on Gian Franco's lap, the next, with a little chirp she'd jump down and race round the apartment, darting up and along the back of the sofa like a crazy kitten. She seemed to Giulia to enter a cat dimension, just out of sight of human beings, whereas Leonardo remained impassively present in theirs. Macchiato was very talkative and determined to make her presence and needs known with a range of sounds from a hiss to a meow to a commanding purr. There was a moment when she gave Leonardo a playful tap on the nose and the Nanninis waited for a scrap. But he seemed too startled to retaliate.

'Torties are very strong willed,' Susan explained when they went to her for advice. 'They're unlike any other cat you'll come across. They're supposed to bring good luck. In America we call them 'money cats.' There's a lovely legend that all tortoiseshell cats are descendants of a black cat that hosted the sun while it walked on the earth. When the sun had to leave the cat's body, it left behind some of its golden rays in the cat's fur.'

That's all very well,' Giulia interrupted. 'But when will these cats get used to each other?'

'It takes time but I'm sure he'll come round. Leonardo has to learn Macchiato's scent. You could swap their blankets for a start.'

'We've done that,' said Giulia. 'Maybe we've done the wrong thing in bringing another cat into Leonardo's territory.'

'Oh, I wouldn't say that, you must…' Susan's voice trailed off. She was staring in the direction of the open doorway. They followed her gaze and saw a well-built man stooping to stroke Shadow, the cat's fur gleaming blue grey in the sunshine.

'Do you think that's him?" Susan whispered.

'Who?'

'The cat poisoner.'

'I'll go and have a word,' Giulia echoed Susan's hushed tone.

They watched as she engaged the man in conversation and saw him spread his arms in a gesture of surprise. She was smiling when she returned.

'I don't think he's our man. He's a retired vet and wondered if there was any way he could be of assistance.'

XXIII

Two days before her trip with Giorgio a strange thing happened. On her way to Largo Argentina, Amy halted in the square and crossed to the La Feltrinelli bookshop. She was gazing at the display of travel guides, planning to buy something on Reggio Calabria, when she became aware of someone standing close beside her. Turning, she saw it was a middle-aged woman. Seconds when she took in the chic cashmere sweater and multi coloured scarf at the woman's neck before she was subjected to an intense scrutiny. The other's gaze travelled over her body, dwelling on her hair, her face, even her shoes, before staring fixedly into her eyes.

'What a pretty woman you are. What a lovely face, and your hair is so beautiful.' Her voice was soft and hypnotic. 'I love that tee shirt you're wearing, it's such a nice colour.'

These exaggerated compliments from a stranger unnerved Amy, she sensed they were insincere and averted her gaze.

'I don't think I know you,' she said.

The other smiled showing brownish teeth. 'Ah but I know you, my dear, the English *gattara* who is interfering in things that don't concern her.' She turned and walked quickly away.

Shaken, Amy took a deep breath and went into the bookshop.

When she arrived at the cat sanctuary she found Concetta in conversation with Stephanie.

'There's been another poisoning,' the Australian told her. 'Not far from Piramide, this time.'

'It was one from my colony.' Concetta was struggling with her tears. 'Chloe, the little tabby, I couldn't save her, she died in my arms.'

'This can't go on.' Stephanie's voice was grim. 'What is this man trying to do? Destroy Rome's cats? He's got to be caught.'

Concetta wiped her eyes. 'Yes, but how, we cannot be everywhere at once and it's a big city.' She broke off. 'But Amy, what is the matter? You look so pale.'

She described the odd behaviour of the woman outside La Feltrinelli, finishing, 'There was something sinister about her. I can't explain.'

The cat lady crossed herself. '*Malocchio*,' she murmured.

Stephanie cleared her throat. 'She's talking about the evil eye. It's supposed to be how someone puts a curse on you, but it's a lot of superstitious nonsense.'

'No, it isn't,' Concetta interrupted. 'It's real. You say she was staring into your eyes? This woman was wishing you ill.'

'But why, I'd never seen her before in my life.'

'Exactly, probably just a bit of a weirdo.' Stephanie busied herself wiping the office table.'

Concetta insisted. 'I'm worried for you, *cara* Amy. There are some in this city who hate what we all do. How do you feel?'

'Fine. It was just a bit unsettling, that's all.'

'Then take care. Accidents can happen.'

'Oh Concetta!' Stephanie sighed. 'What a witch you are! Take no notice, Amy. They're just old wives' tales.'

Concetta left soon after, shaking her head as if to disperse these troubling thoughts. Stephanie opened the logbook to view Susan's entries. There had been two new arrivals that morning and one was distressed. Amy went to check on them and tried to put the incident out of her mind.

XXIV

They could fly to Reggio Calabria and pick up a hired car, but Giorgio suggested they drive down from Rome in a more leisurely way.

'It would give us the opportunity to explore some of the coastline. They call it the coast of the gods and it's considered the most beautiful zone of Calabria. Apparently the views are spectacular.'

After her unpleasant experience, Amy was eager to escape the city for a while and happily agreed to his plan. She was ready and waiting outside the apartment when Giorgio arrived. Above her the sky was pure blue and the sun already warm on her skin. She'd remembered his car had an open top and wore a headscarf and dark glasses.

Giorgio kissed her on both cheeks. He laughed. 'You look very mysterious. Like that movie star, what was her name?'

They left the city and headed westwards. Amy settled back in her seat and enjoyed the ride. But as they neared Naples she grew silent and began to gaze anxiously about her. Suppose Davide were somewhere in the city and saw her with a man? You're being paranoid, she told herself. But when Giorgio suggested they stop for coffee, she panicked and said she didn't fancy the crowded streets and noisy traffic. Couldn't they go somewhere further on?

Soon however she was caught up in marvelling at the long stretch of coast interspersed by jagged rocks, pretty bays and a sea of incredible blue.

'Like it?' Giorgio asked.

'You were right, no wonder it's called the coast of the gods.'

His face lit up in a boyish grin and she thought, he's nice, and I like him. Stop all these suspicious thoughts, Amy.

Their destination was Tropea but they halted several times on the way. At Pizzo Calabro, a typical fishermen's village, they wandered the narrow streets and lost themselves in the labyrinth of alleyways. Climbing upwards, they entered the castle that crowned this place. An air of sadness seemed to linger over the belongings of the once imprisoned King of Naples and they were glad to be out in the sunshine once more. With the help of Amy's guidebook they discovered a little church sculpted from the interior of a grotto where she gazed at the solemn Madonna and child, protector of those at sea. They ate their picnic on a nearby sandy beach, spreading a rug underneath the pine trees.

Amy, gazing over the gleaming white sand and clear water, said: 'you can just imagine Aphrodite rising from that sea.'

'Yes, it is such a romantic place. People have their wedding photographs taken here.' Giorgio poured the last of the wine into their cups and raised his. 'To you, lovely Amy.'

She felt herself blush and bent her head to the guidebook. 'Where are we going this afternoon? The Caves at Zungri sound very interesting.'

Giorgio seemed reluctant to move. He lay back with his hands behind his head, gazing up through the canopy of leaves. Amy felt slightly annoyed and found herself comparing him with Davide who was always eager to make the most of every hour they spent together. She wandered down the beach, marvelling at the eucalyptus trees that appeared to be growing out of the sand. She imagined their roots spreading out beneath her feet, seeking water. When she arrived back, Giorgio was on his feet looking worried.

'I didn't know where you'd gone,' he said. 'Remember Calabria is the last stop before Sicily and the Mafia You must be careful.' He pulled her to him and gave her a hug. 'I'm so glad you're safe.'

She thought, he cares about me, and then, what am I going to do about it?

They packed up the picnic things and drove on. Zungri took Amy by surprise, a step back in time. Set in a landscape of wild grasses and rocky outcrops where the prickly pear reared above them, the whole village was carved from rock and its buildings were almost entirely preserved. The guidebook described how monks had created them and also excavated the rock to allow water to be channelled to each house. Rome seemed very far away.

It was time to move on to Tropea where Giorgio had booked them into the Hotel *Villa Chiara*. Amy followed him up the stairs, wondering what their sleeping arrangements would be. She realised she was relieved when he handed her a key and turned towards the room across the corridor.

'See you in about an hour,' he called over his shoulder. 'There's something else I'd like you to see before we eat.'

She was grateful to be alone for a while. It had been a day of so many new experiences and one she realised had tired her by its intensity. It was also the first time she was going to spend a few days with a man since Davide. Yet Giorgio had been the perfect companion, good-humoured even when they'd been caught in traffic jams. The picnic he'd brought was simple but delicious composed, she guessed, of home cooked food. Perhaps his mother had prepared it? She stirred herself and realised time had passed. There came a knock on her door.

'Ready Amy? We need to get there before the sun sets.'

Puzzled, she followed him out of the hotel to the car. 'Where are we going?'

'*Capo Vaticano*, the last strip of land before the straits of Messina.'

After about twenty minutes the cape could be seen, thrusting from the sea, its white rocks eroded by centuries of breakers, a mysterious place. Giorgio slowly drove the car towards the top where Amy was surprised to see a busy resort. They walked along the narrow streets between small, beautiful houses mantled with colourful plants, then made their way along a path towards the intermittent beam of a lighthouse. It took them along the edge of the cliffs high above the sea. Standing on the rocky bluffs, they gazed over the blue green colours of the water and out into the distance. The view was breathtaking as Giorgio pointed out the silhouette of the Aeolian Islands, the straits of Messina giving onto to Sicily and the lowering bulk of Mount Etna.

She gazed and gazed as if she could never get enough of it. The restless movement of the sea caressing the white sandy beaches made her lose her sense of time. They stood in silence watching while the sky flamed and died to ash as the sun sunk on the horizon.

'I read a legend about a prophetess called Manto who lived in the cliffs of this cape,' Giorgio's voice came to her. 'She gave prophecies in exchange for gifts. Shall we throw something down for her?'

She turned to gaze at his face, indistinct in the twilight. 'Thank you Giorgio, for bringing me here, I wouldn't have missed it for the world.'

He said her name and moving closer took her in his arms and kissed her. After a moment she began to respond, moved by this romantic setting. Then suddenly, involuntarily, the image of the lakeside at Bracciano swept into her mind, Davide's kiss that had told her what she'd longed to know. It had been the pivotal moment that would brook no denial of the strength of their feelings. This felt like a betrayal and Amy pulled away.

As they started back the way they had come, Giorgio said: 'There's someone else, isn't there?'

Amy said nothing.

'Or was, and you haven't got over it.'

She murmured yes, grateful for his perception.

'Do you want to tell me about him?' Giorgio persisted.

Did she? It would be hard to explain. She had known Davide for such a short time and now almost a year had passed since their parting. But a spark of hope had continued to burn, the refusal to relinquish the belief they would meet again. And while that still existed…

'It's not that I don't care for you, Giorgio,' she said. 'I do, I'm just finding it difficult for the moment to…'

Lit only by the now and then sodium lamp showing them the path back into town, they walked in silence or a while. Amy wondered what Giorgio was thinking, whether after this evening he would decide it was all too complicated for them to continue. She was surprised therefore when he spoke

'I understand, Amy. In fact I rather admire you, it shows how deeply you can love, your loyalty, things I like about you. Don't worry, *cara*. We'll just take it easy.'

XXV

'A little gem', the cognoscenti of Saint Michael's called the church in Father Bruno's care. To less observant passers by the exterior had little to commend it, if it were not for the setting: a courtyard garden where a fountain played softly among rose bushes. 'Take a moment to step inside,' he might tell these ignoramuses, 'and you will find hidden treasure: the richly decorated ceiling of a side chapel, glittering mosaics.' In particular, if he scented interest, he would point out a six-winged elaborately plumed angel, the feathers enfolding it adorned with a peacock's all seeing eyes.

This morning he was more concerned by the sight of his cleaner, *Signora* Teresa Mancini, seated in a pew, her head in her hands. At the sound of his approaching footsteps, she rose guiltily to her feet.

'Excuse me, Father, I've only been here a moment.'

'Please,' he indicated for the elderly woman to sit again. 'Is there something wrong?'

She raised her head to gaze up at him. He noticed how pale and strained she looked. 'It's nothing, Father, just a bit of pain in my joints. I'll work it off.'

This wasn't the first time she'd caused him anxiety. On several occasions and without her realising, he had watched her slow movements round the church, the subdued sighs of pain. He sat beside her in the pew.

'*Signora*, perhaps we should have a word. I must ask: is all this cleaning becoming too much for you?'

Her reaction startled him. She jerked away, staring at him with terrified eyes. 'No, Father, no, please don't say that. I love this church with all my heart. I wake every morning and thank the Lord the task has been given to me. Please don't take that away from me.'

'But if it gives you pain.'

'Oh that,' the cleaner dismissed it with a shrug. 'You expect some pain as you get older. But the Madonna gives me the courage to bear it.' She got to her feet. 'Now, Father, if you will excuse me I have the brasses still to do.'

He watched her move stiffly towards the lectern, a cloth and tin of metal polish at the ready. He had noticed recently that her standards had slipped and things were not as pristinely clean as once they'd been. Had her eyes begun to fail her, too? But he could not find it in his heart to tell her to go. Father Eustachio would have done so, he knew. His friend would never accept anything but perfection. Did he minimise his own value by considering the needs and wishes of others? If it was a weakness he couldn't help it, if that was the way he was made. After all the Lord knew his flaws and still called him His perfect creation, "made in his image."

He moved away from the painful sight of his cleaner laboriously polishing the brass eagle and came to a halt by the plumed angel. He read again the inscription at his feet: *He shall cover thee with his feathers and under His wings shalt thou trust: his truth shall be thy shield and buckler*. Father Bruno crossed himself.

He collected some gloves and secateurs and went outside to deadhead the roses. There were eight bushes and he began with the one nearest the church, going down on his haunches to reach the lower branches. The sound of the gate opening disturbed him. He peered round the bush to watch a tall, broad shouldered man enter. He carried a Carrefour shopping bag and made for the place where Father Bruno fed the cats. Here he produced a smaller plastic bag and scattered the contents over the ground. At this Father Bruno shot upright. 'What are you doing?' he shouted. 'Get out, go on get out of here!' The man froze, startled by the sudden appearance of the priest then, with a swift glance behind him at the open gate, made his escape. An inquisitive black cat had appeared and Father Bruno started forward and shooed it away. Gingerly he picked up the scattered food and transferred it to a bag someone had dropped conveniently near the gate. His heart thudded as he imagined what might have been the outcome if he had not been there, for he was almost certain his visitor was the cat poisoner.

XXVI

By some curious chance Giulia and Gian Franco happened to be passing St Michael's at the moment when the man rushed away. They had been keeping their six-monthly appointment with the dentist, only four streets away. Alberto Pino was kindly, middle aged, and skilful at putting his patients at their ease. Giulia, who possessed a healthy mouth of strong teeth, looked forward to the visits. Gian Franco, on the other hand, approached them with dread. Terrified of what new problem *Dottore* Pino would find, he sought excuses for not going, which Giulia killed with a 'don't be a baby.'

'But I clean them twice daily,' he'd regularly protest. 'My wife does nothing more.' It's not fair, he added silently.

'Life isn't fair,' the dentist remarked as he always did. 'You have a natural susceptibility to dental plaque. It is your gums you must pay attention to.'

At each visit, he would demonstrate yet more cleaning devices, each more costly than the last.

When they emerged, Giulia triumphant, Gian Franco demoralised, they would turn away from the hubbub of the neighbourhood, drawn down a cobblestoned lane by the scent of freshly baked dolce. By unspoken consent, Biscottificio Innocenti was always their post-dental stop. Part of the simple bakery's attraction was the huge vintage oven that dominated the centre of the shop. The slow journey of the baking dolce as they travelled the 16-metre conveyer belt was mesmerising. Then there were the biscuits themselves filled with hazelnuts, dipped in chocolate, or covered in jam and almonds. Unerringly, they passed them by to order two slices of the marmalade pie, the latticed pastry revealing its rich filling. It evoked childhood memories for both, of their grandmothers' sweet treat.

Satisfied, they had emerged and begun to make their way back towards Ponte Sisto when the man fleeing the church almost knocked them down. At the same time, Father Bruno appeared in pursuit and, with the dexterity of a footballer, Gian Franco stuck out his foot and tripped the intruder up. For a second he lay on the ground, then struggled up and escaped. In that brief moment, Giulia caught a glimpse of his face and was shocked by what she saw.

'I caught him throwing down food for the cats,' Father Bruno told them. 'By his behaviour, I'm fairly sure it was poisoned.'

'You should have it analysed,' Giulia suggested. 'I suggest you go to our vet, *Dottore* Turiano.'

As they continued on their way, Giulia said: 'I think I recognised that man. He looked very like the one Amy was with at *Pasquetta*.'

Gian Franco halted and stared at her in surprise. 'Giorgio? Oh no, no, you must be mistaken. He's a decent person. He wouldn't do a thing like that.'

Giulia shook her head, murmuring: `remember what I told you? He doesn't like cats. Who knows what a man such as that is capable of doing?'

******

'Oh Father, whatever is going on?' *Signora* Mancini had appeared in the doorway of St. Michael's.

'It's all right, *signora.*'

Some of the cats had appeared and Father Bruno shooed them away, fearful a trace of the poison remained. His heart beat fast at the thought.

'You're pale as a ghost. Come in and sit down.'

In spite of what had happened, he smiled to himself. It was his cleaner's turn to show kindness as she took his arm and guided him into the church.

'I saw him,' he told Father Eustachio when he phoned him a few days later. The results of the analysis had been returned to him. 'The meatballs contained enough rodent poison to kill a colony of cats. Thank God I was there.'

'We might have something more to go on,' was his friend's reply. 'Why don't you come over this evening and we can discuss it further.'

Jennifer Pulling

XXVII

GIULIA 1967

'Don't give up, stay around.' The advice of her mother
was echoed by *Signora* Giordano when, a week after
Marco had told her he was in love with someone else, his
mother invited her to the apartment.

'My son knows nothing of this,' she confided, 'It is
between you and me, you understand?'

Even the discreet Serafina had been banished before
Giulia's arrival. *Signora* Giordano prepared coffee and
set out the pastries herself.

'Apparently, this person is a foreigner and her name is
Carolina. She's supposed to be here studying Italian, but
it's my guess she spends more time ensnaring good
looking young men.' *Signora* Giordano sniffed.
'Especially if they own a Vespa and can show her
around.'

At mention of the Vespa, Giulia felt a pang, recalling
her excursions with Marco. So now another young
woman sat perched behind him, her arms tightly round
his waist as they whizzed through Rome. It didn't bear
thinking about.

'But your son has chosen her over me,' she said,
gazing at the untouched dolce on her plate.

'It's the novelty.' The older woman sounded very sure. 'It will wear off, especially when he realises she can't cook, well…' she smoothed an imaginary crease in her navy skirt. 'Not like a Roman woman can, not like your mother has taught you, I'm sure.'

If Giulia imagined that any failings of the foreigner in the culinary department were more than made up for when it came to sex… weren't all these visitors with their mini skirts and long blonde hair ready to offer that on their second or third encounter, or so she had been told… she remained silent.

'A little adventure and a marriage are two very different things,' *Signora* Giordano lifted the silver coffee pot to refill their cups. 'Believe me, my dear, I am older than you and I know these things.'

Giulia felt a flare of hope that was swiftly extinguished. Whatever became of the liaison with this Carolina girl, Marco had made it clear that marriage was not on the cards with Giulia.

The other's tone sharpened. 'Don't look so miserable, Lia, men don't like it. You must always smile and look carefree.'

But what if I can't, Giulia, thought. How can I when all the time I imagine them together, maybe in that huge bed in his apartment. She, of course, had only glimpsed the bed from the *salone*. She longed to escape this room, this woman whom she was beginning to see in a different light as someone who wanted to control her sons' lives.

No wonder Marco courted freedom and defied his mother, and as for poor Paolo… for a moment she gave a thought to the lengths he went to conceal his homosexuality, and the cruel way his mother held it over him.

The pastries were being offered to her. 'I see you don't like that one on your plate. Have another, the *maritozzi* are very good but so difficult to find, I get them from a little bakery I know.'

Giulia shook her head. She blinked away tears. To her surprise *Signora* Giordano rose to pat her on the shoulder.

'Coraggio, dear Lia, I like you very much and I know you would make a good wife for Marco. Keep strong. We have to fight for what we want.'

As she rode down in the velvet lined lift and was shown out of the building by the supercilious porter, Giulia felt sure the battle was already lost. This was confirmed some weeks later, during which she heard nothing from Marco who seemed to have vanished from his usual haunts. She had been out shopping with *Signora* Giordano who had insisted on buying her a present for her birthday, an expensive silver bracelet. As they neared the Spanish Steps she felt bony fingers grip her arm.

'Look!' The other murmured. 'It's them.'

This was her first glimpse of her rival and Giulia hated her on sight, her blonde prettiness and her long legs. Carolina seemed to be everything she was not. She walked hand in hand with Marco and the couple appeared completely tied up in each other, laughing at some private joke. The next moment they realised they had been seen and Marco put his hand on Carolina's shoulder and turned her abruptly in the opposite direction. But this was not before Giulia had met the foreign woman's gaze and sent a message of utter loathing. It was also the day she knew that Marco was irretrievably lost to her.

XXVIII

The day of their visit to the Museo Nazionale della Magna Grecia where the Riace Bronzes were housed was marred for Amy by an unsettling incident. It happened just after they had arrived in Reggio Calabria and by common consent stopped for coffee. They were sitting in the café's small courtyard shaded by a tree covered in white blossom. Small birds hopped among the branches and one flew daringly close to their table to peck up a few crumbs. Giorgio was studying the guidebook so it was Amy who spotted the small black and white cat slink in from the street and settle near the tree to stare at the birds. Its excited chattering sound made Giorgio look up. He cursed under his breath and stooping, picked up a handful of earth and threw it at the cat, narrowly missing as the animal darted away.

Amy jumped up from her chair. 'What did you do that for?' She demanded.

'It was terrifying those birds.'

'Oh come on, it was only looking. I think it's quite sweet.'

His face was set in a flinty expression that Amy scarcely recognised. She recoiled from him.

When he spoke, his tone was harsh. 'Considering the way you cat lovers gush about your affection for all things sweet and fluffy, it's strange that you can ignore the truth that cats are tyrants who pick on mice, birds and other creatures. Not only do they kill them, they usually play with their prey and torture the poor animals before a slow and painful death. That doesn't sound like sweet behaviour to me.'

She sprang to their defence. 'Cats kill birds because at some point in their existence they needed to hunt to survive. They may have been domesticated but they've kept their predatory instincts. That doesn't mean they are cold-blooded killers.'

She returned to her seat and slumped down, gazing at her empty coffee cup.

After a moment, Giorgio spoke: 'shall we go then? The Museum will be open by now.'

'Go if you want to. I'm staying here.'

'Oh Amy, we haven't come all this way for you not to see them. Come on.'

She shook her head. A wave of panic swept over her. Here she was, far from Rome with someone who had suddenly become alien to her. Her doubts returned that he wasn't the man he'd seemed to be. But she was marooned with Giorgio, in this seemingly outlandish place, unless she could persuade him to take her to a train station. Something of this seemed to communicate to him. He came to sit opposite her and took her hand. 'I'm very sorry. I know how you feel about cats. It was stupid of me. Forgive me.'

Slowly she raised her head from her contemplation of the coffee cup to look at him.

'Forgive me', he repeated. 'I really do want you to see these bronzes. Please, Amy, I beg you.'

In the end she was glad she had relented, it was an awe-inspiring experience. The museum was not as crowded as it might have been at a weekend. As they entered the long exhibition room, empty but for the two statues standing some distance apart on their plinths, they were silent in observation. With their rippling muscles, thick beards and manes of curling hair the bronzes seemed strangely life like. Each struck the same pose, the right leg straight, the left bent.

When Giorgio spoke it was in a whisper 'Some say they were the work of a single artist, others that they were coincidentally victims of a shipwreck and not related at all.'

Whichever, Amy thought, marvelling at the perfection of the two bodies, an ideal masculine form sculpted so long ago. Aware that this might be a unique occasion, they lingered for some time, united in the company of these enigmatic figures, speaking in low voices as if the statues might really overhear. This shared experience diluted the morning's unpleasant scene and, as they emerged into the open air once more, they were discussing where to have lunch.

Next day, their last in Calabria, one they had chosen to spend quietly in Tropea before they started on the journey home, Amy began to feel unwell. First, a strange lethargy crept over her, and then she developed a headache. In the afternoon as they were taking their last stroll she felt suddenly dizzy and had to sit down.

Giorgio insisted they went back to the hotel so that she could rest. She protested she didn't want to waste their last hours in this place, which seemed to have cast a spell on her, exerting a pull composed of charm and a sense of restfulness.

He became unusually firm. 'You might be sickening for something, Amy, or it could even be food poisoning. I was a bit doubtful about those prawns we ate last night, whether they were really fresh. I'll order something bland for dinner.'

The weariness returned and she gave into it, sleeping while the day faded and evening came. The following day there was none of the exhilaration of the journey down and she was glad when they arrived back in Rome and she sought the solitude of her apartment. She made some tea and went to sit at the window gazing down to the square below, but her mind was distracted. She recalled the strange encounter she'd had outside the Feltrinelli bookshop, the woman's fixed stare and her obviously insincere compliments. Could Concetta have been right? Had someone cursed her with the evil eye? No, it was a ridiculous superstition as Stephanie had said. Nevertheless, when she met Paolo the following day and he wanted to hear how the Calabria trip had gone, she broached the subject.

'It was the way she looked at me. I found it difficult to tear my gaze away.'

His expression was serious. 'And this lady, this Concetta suggested she wished you harm?'

'She said it was *malocchio*'

They sat in the Bar Angelo Divino, glasses of wine in front of them. For a while the weariness had lifted and Amy was able to nibble the salami and cheese on their shared plate. Paolo was silent.

'It does sound rather far-fetched, don't you think,' she prompted.

He smiled. 'That may sound so to you, dear Amy, but I can assure you, in Italy, many people believe in it. "There are more things in heaven and earth than are dreamt in your philosophy," as your bard has wisely said.'

'It still sounds like witchcraft!'

Paolo lit a cigarette. 'Amy, haven't you noticed how many people wear a little amulet shaped like a horn? It's supposed to protect them from the evil eye.'

This brought to mind the red horn pendant she had seen at Giorgio's neck. Yet he'd seemed such a rational being. She shook her head in wonderment, which made him laugh.

'You've been here over a year now, *cara*, but there are still many things you have to learn about us.'

Amy considered this, and then remembered her mother's avoidance of peacock feathers in the house. A regular customer of *Zest* had once presented them with three of the bird's feathers, studded with the typical blue eyes.

'Oh they're unlucky, get them out of here,' her mother had ordered, the moment the customer had left.

Was it possible that they were also believed to be agents of the evil eye?

After her meeting with Paolo the malaise seemed to recede for a while. The following morning, Amy was up early preparing *bucatini all'amatriciana* for her taster dish of the day. She had decided it was time to venture into using her spices to copy Italian dishes. After her brief absence, her fellow traders gave her a warm welcome. Salvatore added a brioche to his usual offering of espresso and Matilde enfolded her against her ample form. What fascinated her was that now she noticed both sported the scarlet horn, Salvatore's on a chain round his neck, Matilde's attached to the huge bunch of keys she clipped to her belt.

This gave her the opening she needed to ask: 'tell me, do you honestly believe in *malocchio*?'

Matilde gave one of her expressive shrugs. 'Certainly, why not? There are those in this world who wish us ill.'

'However perfect we are,' Salvatore added. 'It's logical we should protect ourselves. Why do you ask this?'

'Can't you understand, you Sicilian imbecile?' Matilde threw an over ripe tomato at him, which he dodged, laughing. 'Amy is frightened. Has someone put *malocchio* on you, *cara*?'

Amy concentrated on setting out her packets of spices. She was fighting her scepticism. Was this just an Italian superstition and so not relevant to her? And yet… finally she met their gaze. 'I'm beginning to think they have.'

The pair exchanged a glance.

'We can't allow that,' Matilde said. 'You must have it seen to.'

'Oh? How?'

'My mother will sort you out,' the plump greengrocer continued. 'She lives out in the sticks. I'll take you there myself, this Sunday.'

'Out in the sticks' was no exaggeration. Matilde's well-worn car left the main road and took a series of turns down ever smaller roads until they bumped over a stony lane and finally halted outside a ramshackle building guarded by a white dog that barked continually until Matilde told him to shut up.

'You know me, Casanova!' she bent to stroke the animal's rough coat. 'And this is a friend of mine.'

As if he understood, the dog began to yelp with pleasure, his tail wagging furiously. They followed him into the house. A very old woman, or so she seemed to Amy, rose with surprising speed and came to greet them.

'Mamma!' Matilde kissed her on both cheeks. 'I've brought the young lady I told you about.'

Unsure what was expected of her, Amy hung back. It was the other who stepped forward, took her by the shoulders and gazed into her eyes. 'Young lady, what *disgraziata* has cursed you?'

Disconcerted by the woman's dialect not to mention her lack of teeth, she turned for explanation to Matilde.

'She's asking if you have any idea what miserable so and so has cursed you.' She put her hand on Amy's arm. 'No, you don't need to explain. Whoever it was, Mamma can deal with it.'

Amy gazed round the room, noting the fire burning in the grate, though it was a warm spring day. There was little furniture but what there was looked comfortable, if old and shabby. Casanova had jumped up on a chair and settled there. The situation seemed suddenly surreal and she felt a moment of panic as if somehow she would never return to the real world. From the kitchen there was a bustle of activity and then Matilde appeared carrying a bowl of water, which she placed on a table. Her mother sat at it and taking up a bottle of oil, poured a spoonful. Holding it over the water, her lips moved in what appeared a silent prayer, although Amy heard her name murmured. The old woman made the sign of the cross while, with her little finger she let five drops of oil fall into the water.

Matilde let out a long sigh. 'You see, Amy,' she whispered, 'you see.'

Uncertain of what she was looking at, Amy craned forward to watch the oil disperse and mix with the water.

Matilde drew in her breath and murmured 'Ah, *malocchio*.'

I'll wake up in a moment, Amy told herself. The shadowy room, the watchful dog and the murmur of a thick accent had taken on a dreamlike quality.

Again the old woman began a silent prayer and then, approaching Amy, traced a cross several time with her oiled finger on Amy's white tee shirt.

'You'll be fine now,' Matilde told her as they drove away after a prolonged leave taking.

There was no doubt, she felt curiously light hearted. 'It's strange, as if a weight has been lifted,' she admitted.

'And you still don't believe in *malocchio*?' Matilde laughed.

XXIX

Father Eustachio had had a good day, at least as far as God was concerned. In spite of his friend Bruno's reassurances, which had gone some way to restore his faltering belief, he was still prone to the nag of his questioning mind. Today, however, there'd been a sign the Lord might have shown Himself. After morning mass, he had sat for some time in the church, not praying as much as waiting in silence. Time had seemed to stand still and in that moment a sense of certainty had come ever him that he was in the presence of God. He had striven to hold onto this but all too soon it vanished, leaving him gazing round the church as if surprised to find himself there. Nevertheless, he felt energised and in a good mood when Father Bruno arrived bearing two bottles of wine.

'I thought it was about time I contributed,' he said. 'I hope this will meet with your approval.'

Father Eustachio brandished the corkscrew. 'We'll soon find out.'

If this wine was more than a touch inferior to the *Barbera d'Asti* supplied by his merchant, he was not going to mention it. Instead, settled in the study, their glasses before them, he broached the subject of the cat poisoner. 'Young? Old? How was he dressed?'

'I only had a glimpse but I'd say he was in his twenties. He was wearing orange or red trousers but I didn't notice anything beyond that. My fear is that, as he didn't succeed this time, he'll try again and I won't be there to intervene.'

Father Eustachio was considering the wine, with the second glass he came to a decision: this was a *Barbera normale* not a *superiore*. Stop analysing everything, Eustachio, he scolded himself.

'I feel the same,' he agreed. 'Every time I go into the church, I check on St Gertrude. This man must be caught.'

'Yes, and I have an idea. Why not install security cameras then, if we can catch images of him, we'll have some definite proof to take to the police.'

In the silence that followed, Eustachio's expression was quizzical. 'I think it's a good idea,' he said at last. 'Is it legal, though?'

'You might as well ask is it legal to be as curious as a lot of Italians are: looking and pretending not to look, seeing and pretending not to see. Voyeurism is built into Roman architecture; exhibitionism is a side effect of the weather.'

'I'm serious, Bruno.'

'We're just a bit behind other parts of Europe. We don't mind our relatives being nosy but we don't like the idea of authorities spying on us. I suppose it goes back to the days of fascism. But I think we have every right in this case.'

'The end justifies the means? It could be a subject for my sermon.' He was forever searching for inspiration, which Father Bruno usually managed to provide.

'Surely. We are serving a higher purpose in trying to bring evil to justice. You cannot argue with that.' He gave his friend a sly look. 'Shall we have another glass of my less than perfect wine? Oh Eustachio, I can read you like a book. It does not come up to your impeccable standards. But at least it's done the trick, eh? It has brought us to some kind of decision.' He laughed. 'If only by inferior means.'

Father Eustachio joined in his mirth. 'You really are a scallywag, Bruno. Come on, give me your glass.'

XXX

After their trip to see the bronzes Amy told herself she needed to clarify her ambivalent feelings for Giorgio. It would mean choosing to ignore Paolo's remarks about his family and the supposed sightings she'd had of Giorgio, if she were to decide there was any future in their relationship.

When it came down to it, her own family had been less than perfect: an over possessive mother and a father who'd shown little interest in her as a young girl.

It was only after her mother admitted that Bernard had been disappointed in having a daughter and not a son, she'd begun to understand his indifference, knowing it was no fault of her own.

On reflection and to her surprise, she felt reluctant to finish with Giorgio and decided she would give it a little more time. As spring turned into summer they spent several Sundays out of Rome. On one of these, Matilde arranged another picnic, including them now as an accepted couple. It lasted well into the evening with music and dancing under the stars. Giorgio kept his word and dropped her off outside the apartment with just a kiss on both cheeks as he said good night. It was then Amy realised that whole days had gone by without her thinking of Davide. Even the memory of his face and voice, was growing hazy. Guilt swept through her, but however hard she tried to deny it, the acute pain of his absence had gone. She panicked. Had the moment come when he would be consigned to the past?

'How soon until I stop thinking about him altogether?' she asked Giulia.

Following her plaintive telephone call, they'd met in Bar Silvestri, tucked away in a corner although they had to raise their voices above the hiss of the coffee machine and chatter.

'Probably never,' Giulia replied, 'but it will become more a romantic dream rather than a reality. If only Marco had realised that, he might have lived a happier life.'

Amy toyed with her spoon. 'Is that how you think of your time with Marco?'

'More recently, yes. That was thanks to you, or rather when you brought the story of your mother to light again. I realised I'd wasted too many years dwelling on what might have been.' She smiled. 'But he was a lovely man and I've never forgotten him, not after all this time.'

'Even though you've been married all these years to Gian Franco?' Amy persisted.

'Ah, Gian Franco! That's different. Nothing compares with your first love. Was Davide yours?'

'Yes, I suppose… no, I know he was.'

For a moment they were silent, sharing the memory of their first loves, the sense of wonder, intrigue and excitement. It had been innocent, not something they'd tried to do, it just happened.

Giulia said: 'No matter who you love later on, or how you change over time, your first love will always be the first, for the rest of your life. Cherish that, Amy, but don't let it destroy you.'

The following Sunday, Amy met Giorgio in the Borghese gardens. By the beginning of July, summer had truly arrived in the city and they decided it was too warm to risk being caught up in traffic jams as an increasing number of weekending Romans sought the countryside and sea. They found a shady spot by the lake where they sat to watch people rowing their hired boats. The surface of the water sparkled with points of light and gave back to the weeping willows an upside-down facsimile of themselves. They spoke little, just enjoying their surroundings and each other's company. Amy felt at peace with herself. The conversation with Giulia had somehow set her free. After a while they moved on to the café for a cool drink, served by the man she had mistakenly thought to be the cat poisoner.

'How are your cats?' He asked.

'Do you know that waiter?' Giorgio sounded accusing.

'Only because I often have a coffee here when I've been walking in the gardens.'

'Cats, cats, cats,' he muttered under his breath.

'Giorgio!' she slipped her arm through his. 'It's a beautiful day. Let's just enjoy it.'

It was when they stood, admiring the view from the Pincio Terrace, the domes and spires of Rome spread out beneath them, Amy remembered.

'My mother used to come here. She's told me how she used to sit in the gardens and think. She had a lot to think about, whether her love for Marco was strong enough to withstand the Giordano family.'

Giorgio took her hand. 'And do you, Amy? Do you think of your past love? Of Davide?' Did he bring you here?' Again there was a note of jealousy in his voice.

'There wasn't time. We knew each other for so short a while. But I used to come here a lot on my own, last autumn.'

She recalled the strange experience she had had, on one occasion: the apparition of a woman sitting on a bench with a cat on her lap, a woman with a curious resemblance to the statue of St Gertrude of Nivells. Fleeting, but it had filled her with certainty for her future. 'It was here I decided I would stay in Rome, that this was where I belonged.'

His grasp tightened. 'I'm glad, you don't know how much.'

He turned her to him and they kissed. His lips were gentle and she responded, closing her eyes to the moment. That was the day when he broached the subject of his mother.

'She's said she'd like to meet you.'

Amy, recalling how *Signora* Giordano had destroyed her mother's relationship with Marco, was hesitant. 'Your mother!'

Giorgio laughed. 'Don't look so alarmed. I've told you, she's American. She doesn't want to look you over, it's just a friendly lunch. There are no strings, I assure you, my Dad won't even be there.'

It had to come, sooner or later, Amy thought, but was she ready to accept this invitation. Was it another step into Giorgio's world? She was happy, at the moment, to simply enjoy these summer days. Why did things have to change?

He laughed. 'Don't look so serious.'

She stirred herself and managed a smile. 'Ok, tell your mother thanks, it would be nice to meet her.'

They took the tram to Pigneto. Its narrow streets and small shops were a surprise for Amy. It seemed more like a village than a zone that was only a few stops away from the centre of Rome. When they arrived, the daily market was in progress and the area vibrant with different nationalities. A woman in a coral sari was filling her basket with mangoes and other more unfamiliar fruit. The air was filled with the cries of stallholders.

'It's changed a lot since I was a child,' Giorgio told her. 'It used to be a rather dark place, then students from *La Sapienza* moved in and it became much more lively.'

'So you've lived here all your life?'

'More or less, my parents wanted somewhere with a sense of community, a place where the real Romans live.'

They had arrived in Piazza Niccolo Copernico, the area of the *villini*. Giorgio explained: 'These were built for the railway managers and the architect was copying other elegant apartments of Rome.'

Amy gazed at the pink and white liberty style buildings, the tall iron gates confining gardens where lemon trees were hung with globes of yellow fruit. Giorgio's parents had been right, she thought, there was the sense of neighbourhood that reminded her of streets in her hometown.

She followed Giorgio up the white steps of one of these houses. A slender woman in dungarees opened the door. Her long hair was prematurely grey, framing the features of a still young woman.

'Amy!' she clapped her hands together. 'Hi, I'm Chrissie, Giorgio's Mom, so glad you could make it. Come in.'

There was an understated elegance to the interior with its high ceilings, luxuriously covered chaise longue and softly draped curtains, which contrasted with Chrissie's casual appearance.

'Please excuse me,' Chrissie indicated her dungarees. 'I've only just got back from the community centre. We had a bit of trouble with a couple of lads.'

'Mom's anti-establishment,' Giorgio said. 'She and her cohorts take over abandoned factories and work with rebellious kids. It's illegal, of course, but she doesn't care.'

Chrissie gave her son a playful push. 'So was the resistance during the war. By the way, Carlo was hanging around here, today. I've been trying to get him involved in the concert we're doing. I think it would be good for him, but he's… well, you know?'

'I can't imagine why you bother with him.'

'Someone has to.'

Amy sensed Giorgio's unease. 'I'd rather not discuss my cousin, if you don't mind.'

His mother shrugged. 'Please yourself. You don't have to deal with him like I do.'

Amy recalled Paolo's remark about Giorgio's odd family. Had he been referring to Carlo? Her curiosity was aroused.

Lunch was simple, an omelette and green salad followed by cheese and crackers. It was obvious that years of living in Italy had not rubbed off on Chrissie.

'I'm not a lover of pasta, Amy, sorry, especially at lunchtime.' She made a face. 'Unfortunately, my husband thinks he'll die if he doesn't eat it, every day.' She laughed. 'So I say, OK Peppe carry on and see how fat you get!'

'Amy's an experimental cook,' Giorgio said. 'She runs a spice stall and comes up with dishes from all over the world.'

'Mm fried bean burrito with cheese, I adore Mexican food!' Chrissie sighed. 'Amy, you're my kind of woman.'

They smiled at one another and Amy thought: I like you.

When Giorgio went out to the bar on the corner to fetch their espresso, leaving the two women alone, Chrissie said: 'I'm so glad Giorgio has found a friend in you, Amy. Life hasn't been very easy for him, what with one thing and another.'

Did she mean the absent Carlo? Amy longed to question her further.

'Family stuff,' Chrissie added, interpreting her expression. 'When you marry an Italian, you take on his entire family, warts and all. I'd hate my son to do the same thing.'

After lunch, Chrissie took Amy on a brief tour of the community centre. The basketball court was heaving; it looked like two games were going on at once. Teenage boys sat together on sofas, playing a board game. They glanced up and greeted Chrissie by her first name. She was obviously popular.

'A lot of these kids are second-generation migrants,' she said. 'Although their families might have cultural differences, here they all enjoy activities together.'

Giorgio put his arm round her shoulders. 'She's crazy but I love her.'

Chrissie's often sharp gaze softened as she gazed up at her son. He was obviously the apple of her eye. Whatever she said to the contrary, something of the Italian mamma had left its mark on her, Amy thought.

'I told you not to worry,' Giorgio said as they sat on the tram, returning to Rome. 'Mom's a hippy at heart, she just wants people to be free to live by their own lights. My father's learned to go along with it, though I remember rows when I was young.'

They parted at Termini station. Giorgio kissed her goodbye, saying he had calls he must attend to. 'Dinner tomorrow evening?' he added.

Amy was thoughtful as she started on her way back to the apartment then changed her mind. She sat in a corner café watching the early evening rush. Giorgio had said there was no intent in his mother's invitation and yet she had seemed to hint she'd welcome a foreign daughter in law. And then there was the question of Carlo. Amy drained her glass and ordered another. She wanted to stay among people and not be alone with her thoughts.

The telephone shrilled through the apartment when she finally returned. The voice at the other end was faint. It was a moment before she realised it was Davide.

'How are you?'

A series of angry rebukes flashed through her mind. Did he think she put everything on hold until he contacted her again?

'I'm OK, but why have you stayed silent all this time? How do you think I've felt?'

'I know,' he said. 'I'm sorry. I'm surprised you even remember my name, *cara* Amy.'

'Of course I do.' Her tone softened. 'Where are you?'

Instead of answering, he said: 'I've longed to hear your voice, to see you again. I promise we'll meet soon.'

'When?'

'Soon. I'll be in touch.'

As she replaced the receiver, Amy's mind was in a whirl. Her overpowering feeling was anger. How could he expect her to be satisfied by such a brief call and his continued reticence about either his whereabouts or the reason for his long absence? When would he stop this infuriating waiting game? She seized a cushion and flung it to the floor.

XXXI

There were still times when Amy felt like a foreigner in her adopted city, times when she felt alone, isolated and very far from home. There were moments when she realised that she was and would always be, however long she lived in Rome, an ex-pat. On such occasions, she would see clearly that she was not the interesting person she might believe herself to be. She was just foreign.

This had been an emotionally hard week, coping with a sense she found difficult to define until she realised it was homesickness. However hard they tried to include her, friends such as Paolo, Giulia, Salvatore and Matilde were people who felt safe, at home and not 'different'. She missed being among those who might not particularly care about her but where she still felt she fitted in. There would be no need to explain why many things were different in Italy to how they were in England.

It was almost the beginning of June, the month that marked the beginning of summer in the city when azaleas made their yearly appearance along the Spanish Steps. There would be a surge of operas and concerts in and around Rome and the most important of all the festivals: Republic day.

Fifty-two years ago Italians voted to abolish the monarchy deposing and exiling all male members and heirs of the ruling House of Savoy. On 2nd June 1946 the Republic of Italy was born. Its anniversary…

Amy read the entry in her guidebook with a sinking heart. Nostalgic for home, the last thing she wanted was to be caught up in this celebratory fever.

A few days before, she had arrived in Campo de Fiori to find Matilde and Salvatore in a huddle, apparently discussing their plans to secure a vantage point for the festivities. They fell silent when they saw her. Amy began to set out her spices, taking no notice of their now lowered voices until finally they approached her stall.

'Amy *cara*, we wondered if you'd like to join us for our feast in honour of the Festa?' Matilde misinterpreted her blank expression. 'You have no family here and we wouldn't want to think of you all alone on such a day, eh, Salvatore?'

'Certainly not and it would be a sin to miss Matilde's *affogato*.'

Affogato, Amy needed no explanation of this Italian favourite: creamy vanilla ice cream drowning in hot espresso. In her present mood nothing could be less enticing. She had a longing for her mother's blackberry crumble served with hot custard.

After only a moment's pause she said: 'It's very kind of you, but I've already made other plans.'

The pair exchanged a glance.

'Ah, so you'll be with Giorgio's family.'

If they wanted to believe the lie so much the better, Amy thought. She was tempted to add: at least we didn't get rid of our kings and queens, but checked herself.

Giorgio had made no mention of her joining the family meal and she'd presumed they didn't want to include a foreigner on this special day. For this she was grateful. She needed no further excuse to escape the historic centre where the majority of the celebrations would take place. Although she knew that public transport would be reduced, she decided to take the bus to an area of Rome she'd never visited before, Monteverde where the famous Villa Pamphili was situated. There was another reason for this trip, a vague memory of her mother's remark: "an apartment in Monteverde" accompanied by her grimace.

This year the Festival fell on a Tuesday and many of the shops were closed, as was the market in Campo de Fiori. Amy felt like a schoolgirl playing truant as she made her way to Termini Station. Soon after she reached the stop, a queue began to form and when at last the bus arrived she was lucky to find a window seat. As they went on their way, more and more people boarded until the centre aisle was packed with standing passengers, blocking easy exit for those seated. Amy had to fight down a feeling of claustrophobia and, to take her mind off the scent of garlic and tobacco, she opened her guidebook and tried to concentrate. The Villa Doria Pamphili Park was noted for its fountains, lake and statues, she read, but there was more: gardens, waterfalls, ponds and a historical pinewood... so much to see it would fill the whole day. She smiled, congratulating herself on the plan she had made to evade the *Italianess* of the day.

Amy realise the woman seated next to her was gazing enquiringly, misinterpreting her grunt of pleasure. She gave a little nod and was about to turn back to her guidebook when her gaze was riveted on a passenger she could just glimpse some way ahead of her in the crowded bus. His head and shoulders rose above those of the other shorter passengers. His face was turned towards the bus window and with a thrill she realised his profile seemed familiar. Giorgio! Instinctively, she thought it must be him. After the first shock, she tried to rationalise. If it was, indeed, Giorgio, today was a holiday and it was she who had decided to remove herself from the festivities. She had only imagined he would be doing the same as others and spending the day at home with his family. Yet it seemed odd, for Giorgio was conventional in many ways, that he should be taking this bus away from all the celebrations. But that was fine. If he had nothing better to do she would ask him to join her on this trip, it would be more fun to share the day, after all. Excusing herself, she pushed past her neighbour but was then stuck behind a standing couple whose large shopping bags around their feet blocked the way. Before she could squeeze past them, the bus halted at a stop and the man got off. The driver called out to the new, would-be passengers that the bus was full, revved the engine and they were off once more. She tried in vain to see the departing figure before he disappeared out of sight

It wasn't difficult to find her way to the majestic villa, all she had to do was follow the groups disgorging from the parked excursion coaches. A part of her marvelled at the enchanting Secret Garden, its hedges cut into the shape of a dove and a lily. There were exotic plants and flowers and a bronze fountain. But as she stood before the romantic fishponds, her mind returned to the glimpse she'd had on the bus, of the man she guessed was Giorgio. Where was he going, she wondered, gazing at yet more fountains in the adjoining Theatre Garden. By the time she'd reached the palms in the old greenhouses, her mind was distracted by the memory of the tall, well built man she'd glimpsed at the Porta Portese market, the man who had fled from the park. Travelling back on the bus, tired by all the sights she'd seen but also her troubling thoughts, she resolved that the next time they met, she would tax him with these questions. She had to know, one way or the other.

As it happened this turned out to be quite soon. Giorgio telephoned a few days later and suggested another walk in the Borghese gardens. 'I thought we might visit the Gallery, this time.'

'If you like,' Amy said. She wondered if she would be able to concentrate on works of art until, somehow, she'd managed to sort out the confusion in her mind.

As before they sat by the lake and Giorgio took her hand. 'I've missed you,' he said.

Ignoring this, she asked him if he had enjoyed the holiday.

'It was rather boring, to be truthful. You know how I'm not keen on these festivities.'

'I had a nice peaceful day in Monte Verde.' Her tone was defensive.

'I like that part of Rome, those charming art nouveau buildings. You're lucky, you don't have to feel obliged to join in these occasions.'

She said nothing, wondering how he could lie so convincingly.

Giorgio continued: 'Families! Even if my mother doesn't care so much, my father insists we celebrate together.'

Amy met his gaze. 'Oh, so you spent the whole day with them.'

He nodded. 'And a very long day it was. I kept thinking how I'd have preferred to spend it with you. 'Anyway,' he rose. 'It's over now, thank God. Come on, let's go to the Gallery.'

Amy followed him into its cool interior. She felt more mystified than ever.

XXXII

Giulia was preparing a *carbonara* sauce, adhering to the recipe her mother had taught her. Certain rules had to be followed. The meat must be always pork cheek, the cheese pecorino Romano or, at a pinch, combined with Parmesan, raw egg yolks came into it and naturally black pepper. Fortunately it was a straightforward dish, for her mind was elsewhere. She was wondering whether she was duty bound to tell Amy of her suspicions.

'What do you think?' she greeted Gian Franco as he arrived home from the market and plonked his string bag on the table.

'About what?'

'Amy. Should I warn her? The more I think about it, the more I am convinced it was Giorgio you tripped up outside Saint Michael's.'

He cast a look of longing towards the television set, itching to settle down to Rete 4 but his wife's tone was imperious.

'She might be putting herself in danger.'

'Nonsense. I've told you before you can't be sure so why upset her? I wouldn't interfere.'

Their conversation was interrupted by the cats. While Leonardo had apparently decided discretion was the better part of valour, only reacting with a smack of his paw as a last resort, Macchiato had remained hell bent on displaying her tortitude, demanding constant attention. If ignored she would commence her frolics round the room, on one occasion sending Giulia's favourite vase crashing to the floor. The next moment she would curl up on Gian Franco's lap, as if nothing had occurred.

'I think Leonardo enjoys her company in his way,' Giulia would say. 'He's eating much better now, isn't he?'

At a price, Gian Franco thought, mutinously, comparing himself to Leonardo's taking life as it came.

'Don't get me wrong,' he had told his friend, Antonio earlier that day when they met for their habitual coffee. 'I love my wife dearly but she can be perverse at times.'

'What can you expect, she's a woman,' was the reply. 'I never stop thanking my lucky stars I've not been caught in the net.'

Slightly bruised by this remark, Gian Franco replied: 'Oh yes, your mamma has seen to that.'

He had met *Signora* Montefiore once, a stout woman with an incipient beard whose hatred of men, except her son, of course, gave the impression Antonio had arrived by Immaculate Conception.

'Ah my friend,' he continued, 'She won't be around forever. How will you fare then?'

'Mamma will outlive me. She wouldn't dare leave me alone.'

Recalling the essential nature of the woman, he could almost believe Antonio.

Meanwhile the two cats were gradually coming to a rapprochement. When she had tired herself out, Macchiato would snuggle up to the sleeping Leonardo while he made no protest.

'How sweet they look together' Giulia took several photographs to show to *Dottore* Turiano. She returned to the subject of Amy. 'Suppose this relationship develops? Suppose they get engaged? It would be a terrible shock if she found out then.'

Gian Franco eyed the bubbling *carbonara* sauce. He was hungry. 'Found out what exactly?'

'Why that Giorgio is the cat poisoner!'

'Alright, so how are you going to prove it?'

'He dislikes cats.'

'And?'

'It looked like him.'

'You only had a glimpse.'

'It was more the feeling I had, that it was him. Gian Franco, someone who loathes cats is quite capable of killing them.'

Women! Maybe Antonio had a point.

XXXIII

'Well, so you've met Giorgio's mother!' Paolo's eyes sparkled with mischief. 'Things are progressing, eh?'

Amy looked up from the menu she was studying. 'Don't tease me, Paolo. It was only a bit of lunch.'

He nodded but looked unconvinced. Once again they'd met in Trastevere and, seated on the *Basile* terrace, were grateful for the shade of a large umbrella. Passers-by had shed their coats and scarves as an official salute to summer.

'I'm sorry, *cara*, I couldn't resist it. But you got on well? She's a nice, uncomplicated woman.'

The waiter arrived to take their order, which gave the necessary pause to allow Amy to change the subject. 'She seemed worried about the behaviour of Giorgio's cousin… Carlo.'

Paolo's expression changed. 'Ah, Carlo.'

'What is it about him? Has he some problems?'

'Only those of his own making.' He reached for the carafe of wine and poured them both a glass. 'Now that you know of his existence, I will tell you some more about him. He doesn't work, though he gets his money is a mystery. He wanders about Rome day and night, up to no good I'll be bound. He's upset so many people including a friend of mine with the way he carries on. If he has mental problems, the Bevacqua family has always played it down. To my mind he is just a very unpleasant person.'

Amy looked away across the terrace, focussing on a window box filled with scarlet geraniums. 'So when you said Giorgio came from a strange family you meant because Carlo is his cousin?'

'Exactly'

Their first course arrived and they busied themselves shelling king prawns, dipping them into the accompanying sauce. She knew she should be happy, enjoying the meal in her friend's company but she couldn't stop the thoughts passing through her mind. Paolo with his habitual prescience was looking at her enquiring.

'There's something else bothering you, Amy, isn't there?'

She rinsed her greasy fingers in the bowl where a slice of lemon floated, averting her head.

'Yes there is. I've heard from Davide.'

'No! Is that true?'

'He said that we should meet up again soon.'

'And what was your reaction?'

Amy recalled her anger and confusion. 'It was not as I expected. I'd always imagined I'd be overjoyed, not that I'd feel this awful resentment.'

Paolo shrugged. 'I'm not surprised, you've made such progress in moving on, and then suddenly he springs back into your life. Did he give any explanation for his silence?'

Amy shook her head.

'What is your inclination?'

The waiter came to remove their plates. Amy watched him in silence. The memory of Davide, which had seemed to swim out of focus recently, came to her crystal clear. She met Paolo's gaze, aware her eyes were filling with tears.

'I think I know the answer.' His voice was gentle. 'You're still in love with him and you want to see him again?'

She nodded, sighed. 'I do but…'

'You must follow your heart, that's my advice, at whatever cost.'

Amy felt a wave of affection for this man who had become more of a father than her own. 'That's very different from the usual advice I get, which is follow your head, be sensible,' she said.

'Ah but I'm an outsider, *cara*, I'm bound to have different views. I've had many false judgements made of me. I'm always willing to give people a second chance.'

******

With Davide very much in her mind, her first thought when the telephone rang that evening was that it must be him.

'Hello darling.'

With a silent sigh, Amy sank down on the sofa. In no mood to listen to the usual pleas to return to England, she was not prepared for a surprise.

'I haven't rung you for while, Amy. I wanted to do some thinking and I've come to the realisation that it's time I stopped treating you like a child and trying to tell you what to do. You're a grown woman and it seems to me you've been acting very responsibly since you went to live in Rome."

'Mum, it's OK,' Amy began.

'No, let me finish. I'm sorry. I suppose I was trying to tell you to learn from my mistakes but no one can do that. You have to live and learn from your own.'

For a moment Amy was taken aback. Her mother had always seemed to live energetically in the present or was busy with plans in the future. An opportunity offered and she seized it. She was not prone to reflection.

'I've often wanted to ask you, why did you marry Dad? Was that a mistake? You're always arguing with him.'

There was a pause, an inhalation of smoke. 'We're very different people, darling, but he's a good man at heart. He's reliable and he's given you and me a lovely home.'

'But you didn't love him like you loved Marco, did you?'

It was the first time they had broached the subject of her lover and Amy heard an intake of breath. She imagined how her mother would stub her cigarette in the scallop shell she always used as an ashtray and consider lighting another one. In that moment her heart softened as she realised what her question had stirred.

'You're right, it was nothing like my feelings for Marco. I loved him with all my heart. I believed he was the man I wanted to be with for the rest of my life. I fought hard for him but there were forces that were far too strong for me to win. I vowed I would never go back to Rome, but you cannot imagine the pull it had over me for quite some time. Marco wrote and tried to persuade me that things could work out and, if I'd let my heart rule my head, I would have believed him.'

'But you got over it? And then you met Dad?'

'Yes, I met Dad and when you were born it all seemed to have been worthwhile.'

Amy had a sudden longing to feel her mother's arms round her, and hear her say the words of her childhood: "it will all come right, you'll see."

'Oh Mum, I'm sorry I'm not there.'

Her mother's voice strengthened. 'No Amy, I will not be selfish any longer, pestering you to come home. It has

175

been very wrong of me. I can tell you are happy in Rome. You *are* happy, darling, aren't you?'

She longed to spill it all out, to have someone else share the weight of her conflict. 'Yes, just one or two decisions to be made, but I promise I'll come back more often to see you in future.'

'That would be lovely, darling. But remember I am not going to pressurise you.'

Amy replaced the receiver happy about this new more equal relationship between them but she was intrigued as to what had caused such a change of heart. Had her mother, in an unusual mood of soul searching, mused on her past travel loving days?

But her decision remained to be made.

XXXIV

A postcard from Davide arrived the following morning. On her way out to the spice stall, something prompted her to check her mail. She recognised his handwriting at once.

I will see you this coming week.

Amy stared at the row of residents' letterboxes, trying to take it in. Once again he had upset her equilibrium and, once again her first reaction was irritation. He seemed to be playing a tantalising game with her and she was growing tired of it. Throughout the morning as she smiled and talked to customers, her mind was in turmoil. It wasn't fair. He hadn't even said which day. Did he expect her to wait in a vacuum, to be content with these occasional messages and vague promises? She found she was justifying a decision to accept Giorgio's invitation to his father's birthday party. But supposing? Be strong, she corrected herself. She caught Matilde's enquiring eye and realised she had spoken aloud.

'Just some difficult decisions I have to make,' she explained. 'Between one thing and another.'

'Ah decisions how I hate them! Whichever I choose I always think I am wrong. Jump at it as if you were diving into cold water, that's my advice.'

That evening Giorgio seemed to have assumed she would join the party. He told her how much his mother was looking forward to seeing her again. 'I'll pick you up around seven, if you can be ready by then.'

For a moment she wavered. Shouldn't she stay in the apartment, waiting in case Davide arrived? Or more probably did not, she corrected herself and banished the thought.

'Yes that's fine,' she said.

'There'll be quite a lot of us,' Giorgio warned her. 'Dad has a large family so Mom insisted we held the party in a restaurant. She said she could never cater for a crowd.' He laughed. 'Cooking isn't her strong point.'

A long table covered by a white cloth had been set outside and most of the family were seated by the time they arrived. She caught several questioning glances and wondered how she was going to deal with the Italian inquisitiveness she had come to expect. Chrissie seemed to realise she was nervous and broke off her conversation to come over to her.

'It's lovely to see you, Amy. Come and sit by me.' She lowered her voice 'I know how you feel, but don't be shy, they're really quite harmless.'

She was greeted by smiles as Italian hospitality took over, one passing her bread, while another filled her glass. It became obvious Chrissie had prepared them. She was made to feel she was the star guest.

'You run a spice stall?' an elderly man said. 'Ah I remember some wonderful curries when I was in India.'

His wife gave him a little push. 'You and India! Do you know, Amy, he has never forgotten his time there. I'll have to send him to your stall for instruction.'

Her husband grunted. 'Good idea, my dear, you could never cook curry. Believe this, Amy? She gives me spaghetti every day of my life.'

There was laughter and cries of shame and Amy joined in. After two glasses of a good wine she had begun to relax.

To Amy's relief the *anti pasto* and first course were followed by a light *caponata* of aubergine and courgettes. As they started on the first course, she felt the nudge of someone's elbow. It was the small, thin woman seated on her left.

'I hear you also work with the street cats?' she murmured. 'I have two at home. Tell me about them.'

Amy turned to her with a smile. But before she could speak, Giorgio broke in.

'Not now, for heavens' sake! Once Amy gets going on her beloved *mici* she'll never stop.' He reached across the table to tap her hand and continued: 'I really think she loves them better than me.'

She felt a stab of annoyance at the jealousy in his voice.

'I'm sorry,' the small woman murmured. 'I didn't mean…'

Amy turned to her. 'Perhaps you'd like to come to Largo Argentina and meet some of them.'

The moment passed and as the evening progressed and she drank more wine than usual, the faces round the table appeared to her increasingly likeable. She felt she was being embraced by this new life, accepted by Giorgio's family and that it wouldn't take more than a few steps to belong. She caught his eye and wondered if he was thinking the same. I don't love you, she thought, but I do like you a lot. Perhaps that is enough. I am tired of being alone.

When later they walked to Giorgio's car, she stumbled a little and he caught her arm.

'I think you are a little drunk!' he said.

'What if I am? I've enjoyed myself, this evening.'

'I'm so glad. The family liked you.'

'And I liked them.'

He laughed and pulled her to him. He stroked her hair back from her face and kissed her. 'And I love you, dear Amy, very much. My aunt asked me whether we were getting engaged.'

Amy giggled. She was, she realised, more than a little drunk. 'Who knows, Giorgio? It's not impossible, is it? Nothing is impossible, this evening.'

Realising he would get little sense out of her, he smiled and opened the car door and helped her inside. 'Let's just get you home.'

She was almost asleep, leaning on his shoulder, by the time they reached the apartment. Gently he eased her upright.

'Tonight isn't the right time, Amy, but soon can we talk about getting engaged?'

Too tired now for any further discussion Amy agreed, kissed him on the cheek and got out of the car. He waited until she'd reached the door and then drove away.

It was as she was fumbling with the key in the lock she felt a light tap on her shoulder. She gave a little scream. Turning round, she saw it was Davide.

'You! I can't believe it,' she said.

'I've been sitting in my car waiting for you to come home. Where have you been?'

'To a party, I am allowed to live, you know?

'And who was that man?'

How much had he seen, she wondered. 'Just a friend, he offered me a lift home.'

'Is that all?'

She felt guilty for lying but his presence was overpowering. 'Yes.'

'Well you certainly couldn't have got home on your own.'

'Are you saying I'm drunk?'

He laughed for the first time, the low laugh she remembered. 'Let us say just a little tipsy.'

There was something different about him, he seemed older and thinner.

'Davide, what is it?'

'There is something I need to explain to you.'

What could be so important that he seemed to be holding back from kissing her? Was he ill? She queried.

'No, but a little sick of life without you.'

'Oh Davide.' She felt such a physical longing for him, but he took the key from her, opened the door and pushed her gently inside the hall. He made no move to follow her.

'The day after tomorrow,' he was saying. 'I'll come about eight.'

He was gone and in a daze. Amy let herself into the apartment. Would the mystery of Davide never end?

XXXV

With a certain amount of trepidation, Father Eustachio made his way to Termini station where he had arranged to meet Bruno. He had spent a night of fitful dozing interspersed with worrying whether what they were embarking on was strictly legal. Surely there was some rule about invading people's privacy in setting up this security camera thing? At very least, shouldn't they obtain a licence?

His friend had brushed all this aside. 'A mad man is out there killing cats, defacing holy statues! Do you want to catch him or not?'

'Of course I do but surely the police…?'

Father Bruno thrust his chin forward and up, mouth pulled down. 'Boh!'

'I know you don't want to talk about it. Once you've made up your mind there's no budging you.'

His friend spread his hands. 'Yes, or no, or do you want to go on discussing it for another month? Really Eustachio, you are an old woman, at times.'

This was possibly the nearest the two priests had come to a disagreement in all their years of friendship. They glared at one another and then Father Bruno let out a bellowing laugh. Still quivering with mirth, he took Father Eustachio by the shoulders and smiled into his face.

'Don't worry so much, old chap. This is Italy! Sooner or later things sort themselves out.'

Nevertheless, the anxious priest was feeling fragile as he stood in the entrance to the station. The moment his friend arrived he would suggest an espresso before they started their journey.

The Tiburtina train was waiting. Their destination was *Trony* where Father Bruno bought all his electrical appliances. All the assistants knew him and greeted him with a wave. Father Eustachio felt dazed by the image of a group of dancers multiplied myriad times on the illuminated screens. He blinked when a young man approached him to ask if he needed assistance and nodded towards Father Bruno.

'You'd better talk to him.'

The young man's black curls danced and his brown eyes shone when he learned they were shopping for a security camera. The decade had seen a leap in popularity, he told them, and digital versions had been introduced as opposed to the old analogue camera. It was all very exciting.

All Father Eustachio wanted to do was buy the thing and escape from this brightly-lit place with its jungle of electronic devices. He had no inclination to examine the advances of technology or to have the niceties of analogue versus digital explained, even if he could understand what the devil they meant.

Father Bruno, on the other hand, had been caught up in the assistant's enthusiasm and had followed him to the section of the store where security cameras were situated. Reluctantly Father Eustachio joined them as his friend asked his first question and the young man looked incredulous at his ignorance before beginning an explanation.

'The main function is to capture light and convert it into a video signal that can either be displayed on a screen or recorded. Up until recently, the traditional camera, the analogue, has been used but now things are changing and with the arrival of digital... well!'

It was obvious from his expression he interpreted analogue as tediously familiar and was eager for customers to share with him in embracing the digital age. This made no impression on Father Eustachio who had considered his thirty-two inch television set quite adequate for the past ten years. As for possessing a mobile phone! If people wanted to contact him they could so at home. The idea of a priest walking through the streets with that object clamped to the ear he found most undignified.

Meanwhile Father Bruno was pursuing the digital route and if he didn't quite grasp the acronyms the young man was firing at him, the VCRs, DVRs and IPs, he wasn't letting on.

Encouraged the assistant continued: 'another recent innovation is the digital multiplexer, which allows a digital video recorder to simultaneously record video from more than one security camera.'

At this point Father Eustachio gave up. His thoughts returned to the dream he'd had at one point during his anxious night. He was standing in his church before the statue of Gertrude of Nivells. As he gazed, her lips moved and she addressed him, asking what was giving him such anguish of the spirit. It seemed quite natural to reply: 'I think I'm going mad' He felt the light touch of her hand on his bowed head and heard her voice. 'Not mad, just a traveller who has lost his way. But soon the path will open up to you again and the desire of your soul will find God.' He had woken to find tears on his face. But the essence of the dream had stayed with him, its assurance that somehow he might find his way back to the Lord.

Father Bruno and the young man were eyeing him enquiringly. He stirred himself and enquired if they had come to a decision.

His friend looked shamefaced. 'After all this I've decided we'll go for the simplest camera coupled by a cable to a display monitor. It's affordable and a do it yourself self-contained system. We can always update,' he added, catching sight of the assistant's crest fallen expression.

A wad of lire notes exchanged hands. The brown eyes pleaded but failed to sell them an extended warranty. The assistant shrugged his shoulders and saw them to the door.

Father Eustachio watched while his fellow priest installed the camera.

Every so often, he glanced anxiously behind him, fearful someone might be watching. He was still not convinced that what they were doing was legal. Did the ends always justify the means? Father Bruno had no such qualms.

'There!' He rubbed his hands gleefully. 'All done. Now let's see what we can net!'

With a thermos of coffee and a hearty panino supplied by his housekeeper, Father Bruno camped down in the church. Father Eustachio took his leave, warning him to be careful. To his horror, his friend produced a pepper spray from his cassock pocket.

'Bruno!'

'It is legal to possess one.'

'Yes, but to use one?'

'Don't be such an old woman. This maniac must be stopped.'

Eustachio decided to abandon his companion to his new toy.

It was quite an education, Bruno thought, seeing what happened in the garden as night came. A plump boy seated himself on the bench to scoff a large slice of pizza, a man and woman wandered among his roses, gesticulating in what looked like a row, a courting couple… tactfully he turned his gaze away. At last the garden seemed to settle down for the night. He finished his coffee and thought about going home. A moment later he was alerted by another image, fuzzy it might be but it was definitely a tall, broad shouldered man. Clutching his pepper spray, the priest sprang into action.

Meanwhile, a sense of guilt was still troubling Father Eustachio, he let himself into his own church and knelt before the Christ. He prayed 'Father free me from my doubting mind. Let me be trusting as Bruno is trusting. Let me be clear eyed in seeking justice as he is.' He waited. He prayed again. Nothing. Silence fell as tangible as the dark shadows in the side chapel as night came on. Finally he got to his feet and trailed down the aisle, feeling peculiarly weary. He would ignore his usual habit and have some coffee before he went to bed.

It was as he stood in the brightly lit kitchen, waiting for the coffee to percolate, he thought he heard a voice deep inside him: *I'm not going to take your doubts from you but I'll walk in the dark forest with you through it.*

Had he imagined it? He felt a shift inside him that convinced him it might true.

XXXVI

It was that hour in the July afternoon when the city seemed to be holding its breath. Tourists straggled through the streets in dogged pursuit of culture, their hands grasping guidebooks sticky with sweat. Most sensible Romans were still in a state of postprandial lassitude with the blinds drawn against the heat, or sitting in the shade of café umbrellas. The English cemetery, a field of wild daisies at this time of year, was practically deserted. This silence and stillness emphasised the utter abandonment of the Angel of Grief on Emelyn Story's tomb, throwing herself with drooping wings and hidden face over a funeral altar. Cats slept in the shade of the greatest tomb of all, the pyramid, but not Concetta.

In the shade of the little gazebo she had set up she was busy washing feeding bowls and preparing her colony's evening meal. By her side her new companion waited patiently. Tiger, a large Bengal cat, had been dumped at her sanctuary some weeks previously. Like all felines of his breed, he was very active and Concetta guessed his energy had proved too much for his owners. For a time he had mewed piteously as if he missed his home, then one day seemed to decide she was the next best thing. Since then he followed her wherever she went. She was stroking the bold marbling and spotting on his thick, lustrous coat when she felt his body grow tense. 'What's wrong Tiger?' He ignored her, staring ahead, his ears laid flat back on his head, making a growling sound. Concetta sensed an atavistic fear of danger. She seized the walking stick she used occasionally and stepped out into the sunshine. Dazzled for a moment, she screwed up her eyes then looked again. A few yards away, a tall man with his back to her was emptying the contents of a plastic bag over the ground. Heedless for her own safety, Concetta rushed forward, brandishing her stick. She was no match for him and he wrested it out of her hand and threw it away. At that moment something streaked past her and with a bloodcurdling yowl Tiger leapt and with extended claws raked the man's bare leg. He cried out in pain and bent to examine the wound. Tiger struck again, this time his aim was the man's face. Blood half-blinding him, the man stumbled away and disappeared.

'In all my time as a cat lady I've never seen anything like it,' she told her fascinated audience the following day. She had arrived at the cat sanctuary when Amy and Stephanie were on duty to relate what had occurred. 'That cat was more like a dog and completely without fear. He seemed to be protecting me.'

'And you think that man was the poisoner?'

'What else was he doing there scattering food all over the place?'

'I suppose he could have been a tourist thinking he was helping?'

Concetta was adamant, something about his sly behaviour had convinced her.

Stephanie asked: 'Did you save any of the food?'

'Good Lord no, I got rid of it as soon as I could.'

Amy didn't add it might have been analysed for its contents. In Concetta's state she would probably have done the same. The little cat lady seemed disorientated and kept repeating: 'what a cat! Have you ever heard anything like it?' Stephanie fetched her a coffee from a nearby café and made her sit down to drink it. After a while, Amy went back to her afternoon's chores combing the tangles of a neglected Persian cat whose fur was badly matted. The killer might have been frightened off but they were still no further in tracking him down.

She thought no more about it until the phone rang in the apartment, as she was getting ready to meet Giorgio. He was apologetic. 'I'm sorry it's such short notice, Amy, but I have to take Carlo to hospital.'

She had been looking forward to this day at Fregene, to relax on the beach and escape the city's ever-growing heat. Damn Carlo!

'Oh, so what's wrong with him then?'

'He has a badly infected scratch on his cheek. He needs to see a doctor. Apparently he was out in the country helping my uncle clear some undergrowth on his farm. He has a nasty wound on his leg as well which needs looking at'

'I see,' she said as calmly as she could manage: 'You'd better take some photographs of those scratches then, in case your uncle needs to claim insurance.'

'Oh Amy, do you think that's necessary?

'Yes, I do. It might be more serious than you think,' her tone was cryptic. 'In fact would you like me to bring my camera?'

'If you don't mind.'

An idea was gradually forming in her mind. Two scratches, just as Concetta had described, surely it couldn't be a coincidence: Was Carlo the cat poisoner? Were the sightings she'd had of supposedly Giorgio his unpleasant cousin, to whom he bore a resemblance? She tried to keep any emotion from her voice, although excitement was building within.

'No, not at all.'

'I'll pick you up in about twenty minutes.'

As they waited to see the doctor, Amy's thoughts continued. Now that she saw the two together she realised there had been something different about the man she'd seen, subtle but apparent if she'd only recognised it, instead of jumping to conclusions. Carlo was slightly shorter than Giorgio and more thickset. His features might have a superficial resemblance but were coarser. He smelt, the unpleasant acidic odour of someone who hadn't washed or changed his clothes. Although she had never seen him close before, as she met his gaze she thought she saw a flicker of recognition before he turned away to speak to his cousin. Amy noticed that there was a crusted red bump on the site of Carlo's facial injury and took a quick photograph. She recalled the vet at Largo Argentina lecturing them on the potential hazards if a cat scratched you, the particular risks with a reduced immune system. Bacteria could spread to the lymph glands and fill them with pus. If neglected it could be fatal.

When the doctor arrived to examine Carlo she was watchful. 'He doesn't look very well,' she told Giorgio as his cousin was led away for tests.

'He'll be OK. He's used to getting bites and scratches when he's working with my uncle.'

Are you sure that's how it happened?' she persisted.

'Of course, how else?'

Amy had noticed Carlo's soft, unused hands, the manicured nails 'He just doesn't look like someone who does manual work.'

'Amy, what are you suggesting?'

She didn't answer, her mind busy with the sites of Carlo's wounds, the symptoms they implied. Images flashed through her mind of cats suffering the death agonies of poisoning, the distraught features of Concetta who was helpless to save her little tabby. She could scarcely contain her anger.

'You do know he's a damaged person,' Giorgio tried. 'He had a violent father and his mother committed suicide.'

She spoke through clenched teeth. 'I don't care the hell about Carlo's childhood,' she replied. 'He is a nasty, cruel man.'

He was silent, gazing at her as if she'd suddenly become a stranger. Amy glared back at him.

'I can't understand why are you're being so offensive?' he said, at last. 'What has Carlo done to you?'

The return of his cousin accompanied by a nurse interrupted this.

'Doctor has taken blood tests,' she told them. 'He will need to measure antibodies to a bacteria in the blood. Please be patient, it may take a while.'

'Do you know which bacteria?' Amy asked.

The nurse was already moving away. 'Possibly bartonella,' she called over her shoulder. 'We'll see.'

Bartonella, the word ballooned in her mind as they waited for what seemed ages, watching other people come and go, making desultory conversation.

Carlo hunched in his seat. 'I don't know what all this fuss is about,' he growled. 'A simple scratch! Why don't they just dress it so I can go home?' He appealed to his cousin, ignoring Amy.

Giorgio glanced from one to the other, obviously bewildered as to what was going on. 'I don't understand either. Do you, Amy?'

She nodded.

'What do they think those blood tests will show?'

Amy said: 'Probably that Carlo didn't get those scratches on the farm.'

Giorgio clicked his tongue. 'Stop speaking in riddles, Amy.'

'Why don't you go,' said Carlo. 'There's not much point in three of us waiting.' He seemed anxious to be rid of them.

His cousin glanced at his watch. 'You're probably right.' He turned to Amy. 'It's too late to go to Fregene but we could do something nearer Rome. What do you think?'

Amy's tone was grim. 'You go. I'm staying here. I want to hear the results.' She could see by Giorgio's expression he was exasperated.

He got to his feet. 'Very well, if you insist.'

They watched the retreating figure. After another half hour the nurse returned to take him to the doctor's consulting room. She seemed to assume Amy was a relative and made no objection when she followed them.

'The bartonella bacteria has shown up in your blood' the doctor said. 'These things usually clear up on their own but the sites if the scratches do look infected. Nurse will give you an antibiotic shot and then you can go home.'

'Carlo said: 'I don't need antibiotics.'

The doctor smiled as if he were addressing a child. 'Allow me to know better, Signore Bevacqua 'I'm afraid I can't discharge you without the medication.'

Amy watching Carlo's reaction was intrigued. Wide eyed he was looking round the room like a trapped animal.

The nurse spoke gently. 'Just roll up your sleeve for me, please. It won't hurt.'

Carlo's arm was reluctantly revealed, pallid as if it never saw the light of day. There was something else mapping the skin: fresh bruises and marks that looked like light pink scars covered the area over a vein.

The nurse had seen it too. Stony faced, she ushered them from the room and told them to take a seat. As the door closed behind them, she heard the murmur of voices.

Carlo said: 'I'm thirsty. Why don't you make yourself useful and get me a coke?'

Amy stared at him. 'No,' she said.

'Bitch!' he muttered.

Her Medusa glare could have turned him to stone. 'You did it, didn't you, Carlo?' she spat his name. 'You murdered those defenceless cats.'

He shrugged. 'You're a crazy woman, Amy, you and your wretched cats. They're pests those animals and I know Giorgio agrees with me. I don't know why he bothers with you.'

'I know you did it,' she persisted. 'Bartonella bacteria, you heard what the doctor said: cat scratch disease, that place on your cheek is a symptom and I have it all recorded here.' She got to her feet. 'Now I'm going to leave you to deal with the doctor and go to the police.'

He gave a snarl like an enraged animal and made a grab at her camera but she dodged out of his way.

'Anything wrong?' A passing male nurse asked. 'Is this man bothering you?'

'I don't think he's feeling well.' She pushed past him and hurried down the corridor. 'Excuse me, I have a pressing engagement, can't stop.'

First of all, she must call Giulia.

XXXVII

Gian Franco, immersed in the *Il Messeggero*, was startled to see his wife standing in the middle of the room, fists clenched, muttering: 'Yes, yes!'

'What's up?'

Giulia turned to him. 'What's up? Amy has only discovered the identity of the cat poisoner.'

'Are you sure?

'Yes, and I'm meeting her to make a *denuncia*.'

'And your evidence?' Gian Franco was a fan of Andrea Camilleri's fictional detective, Salvo Montalbano. He could hardly wait for the books to be televised.

''Certainly, cat scratches on his leg and face.'

'Circumstantial evidence, Giulia.'

She glanced up from putting on her outdoor shoes. 'Don't play the detective with me, my dear. The man has cat scratch fever, quite badly it seems. He's being treated with antibiotics. As a rule I wouldn't take that Piramide cat woman's word as gospel. But if Amy is convinced, then so am I.'

XXXVIII

In a brief telephone call, Davide confirmed he would come to the apartment at eight the following evening. Twenty-four hours of anticipation in which Amy pondered the possible outcome of this meeting. From his tone she guessed it was going to be decisive to their future.

She met her anxious expression reflected in the mirror, regretting the contrast of her feelings from their first date just over a year ago. She had felt a different emotion then, exhilarated with the promise of romance. She'd been a little disappointed that he'd planned only local sightseeing. But Davide had showed her another side of Rome. At one point he'd given her his handkerchief to wipe a blob of ice cream from her face. She still had it and often wondered at the embroidered two initials, even now, she didn't know his surname. Would he divulge the reasons for his secrecy tonight? Did she want to know them?

An hour before he was due to arrive she was roaming the apartment, straightening a cushion, tweaking the flowers she had arranged in a vase. She'd bought a special wine but wondered now if this was to be a happy occasion or would it only disillusion her further. She paused again to gaze into the mottled glass of the old mirror. 'Calm yourself,' she scolded. 'This is Davide who is coming, the man who told you he loved you.' She eyed the frilly sleeves and low neckline of her summer dress and found herself wondering whether she should have chosen something more formal. Anyway, it was too late to change, the intercom buzzed and, heart racing, she opened the door to Davide.

He gazed around the apartment as if reacquainting himself with it. 'It looks different somehow,' he said. 'Not as I remember it.'

You too, Amy thought. Like her, as time went by the edges seemed to have blurred for him, too. She guessed he'd found it hard to picture this place.

'It's the same as when you were here last,' she said. 'I haven't changed anything.'

'Yes, I suppose it is.' He wandered over to the dresser and picked up a small china figure of a cat. He turned to smile at her. 'So you haven't stopped being a cat lady!'

The ornament had been a peace offering from Giorgio after their falling out in Reggio Calabria.

'Oh, no.'

'And Shadow, is he OK?'

She nodded. There was a lump in her throat and she wanted to cry. She longed for things to be as they were but instinctively felt that time had passed. There seemed to be a barrier between them, a sense Davide was keeping up his guard.

She indicated the kitchen. 'Would you like a drink? Wine? Coffee?'

'Wine, thank you, if it's not too much trouble.'

It was the politeness of a stranger. The tension was becoming unbearable. She managed a laugh. 'Oh Davide, of course it isn't too much trouble. It's wonderful to have you here.'

Seating herself beside him, she pleaded: 'Please tell me what is going on.'

His expression softened and he murmured her name. He took her into his arms and she felt the familiar firmness of his body. As she smelled his cologne, a sense of joy rushed through her. In that moment, all the fears and doubts of the past months dissolved. She had come to safe haven. But all too soon the moment passed and he drew apart and reached for his wine. Her joy was replaced by bewilderment.

'Davide?' she whispered, 'what is it?'

At last he spoke. 'Amy, I've kept you in the dark long enough, it's time you knew the whole truth.'

The story he told was something she could never have imagined.

'In 1992 I was at university in Palermo when, one day, my life completely changed. I was at my then girlfriend's birthday party. Her father was the head of the Palermo police. We were all enjoying ourselves when news came of the bomb blast, which had killed the anti Mafia judge Falcone, his wife and security officers. Everyone left in tears. I got on my motorbike and drove to the centre of the city to see how people were reacting. I saw a group of men sitting in a bar, laughing and joking while they ate their *panini*. I went up to them and told them Judge Falcone had been killed. Do you know what they said? "What the hell do we care?".'

He paused to refill their glasses.

'Go on,' Amy urged.

'I don't know what came over me but I was at once certain of what I needed to do. The following day I applied to join the Catturandi, the special police force. I wanted to catch those men who had committed these terrible crimes. The job was dangerous, very few young men like me wanted to join so I was readily accepted.'

He sipped his wine. 'You know, this is excellent.'

Where was all this leading? Amy asked herself. She was on edge, waiting to hear the rest of this story.

Davide continued. 'When others of my age were going to nightclubs I was trailing Mafia bosses like Giovanni Brusca. He was the man who murdered Falcone. We tracked him down and arrested him the year before I met you.'

He paused and took both her hands in his. 'Tesoro, you turned my world upside down. I tried to keep my distance, I was afraid of exposing you to the dangers I was facing, but I couldn't help myself falling in love. In the end, I decided the only thing I could do was take myself away and try to forget you.'

In the silence that followed, Amy tried to absorb this turn in events.

'So why are you here now?' she asked, at last.

'Because however much I try to convince myself it is best for both of us, I cannot forget you, my darling. You have become part of me. My dearest wish is that we could be together for always. At the same time, I know I'd be endangering your life as well as my own.'

She saw in his eyes the weight of the conflict he was facing. She remembered how he had struggled with himself during the short time they'd been together. The pieces were falling into place.

His grip tightened. 'Never feel guilty if you decide I ask too much. Of course I would understand.'

'Don't!! Amy cried. 'All I know is I can't bear to lose you again, Davide.'

He wiped away the tears coursing down her cheeks. He held her tenderly. 'Darling, I beg you, think it over. This is a very big decision, don't make it right away.'

His nearness coupled with nostalgia for what had existed between them overcame her. She continued to weep. 'Don't leave me, Davide. Stay with me tonight.'

In the shadowy bedroom lit now and again by a passing car, where the sounds of the city were muted they stood a little apart, shy of one another. She wondered if the magic that had existed between them had evaporated. There was none of the eagerness of before. Davide took a step closer and gently caressed her face.

'You've changed,' he murmured.

She smiled. 'I'm a year older.'

'No, not that, I mean you are different somehow, I can't explain it.'

So are you, Amy thought, was this what happened when the flame of love wasn't tended? Again she wondered if the time apart had eroded their sense of oneness.

Gently he kissed her and she responded, tenderly at first but then more urgently. 'You know I love you,' he said.

'Yes, I know.'

Naked now, their bodies fitted as they always had in the past. He laid her down on the bed and leant over her with kisses. His lips were firm and strong and she opened her mouth to him, feeling her body softening, yearning for his. She held up her arms to him and drew him down.

But all was not quite as before. The present and its hazards remained with them, competing with their pleasure as they came together in a moment of surrender. It was as if there was a third presence, an undertone reminding them that beyond these walls death and violence lurked, preventing the pure union of the past. Afterwards, they regarded each other ruefully like two players aware they have not given their best performance.

'I'm sorry,' he said.

'Why sorry?'

'To lay all this on you.'

Amy smiled. 'I'm glad you have. At last I know who you really are.'

He kissed her. 'In love with you.'

They laughed, embraced and were now content in each other's presence. And so the night continued, a tender reunion until they fell asleep in each other's arms.

In the early morning, as she watched fingers of light creep into the room, Amy considered the implications of all he had told her. The euphoria of being together again had begun to fade and in its place the reality of the decision she must make took hold. She gazed at him sleeping peacefully as if without care and wished he would not wake, not yet. She didn't want the day to start with its complications. She left him and went to make coffee. While it percolated, she stared round the kitchen marvelling at its ordinary sameness when her world had shifted in the past few hours. When she returned he was putting on his clothes. He turned from the mirror to take her in his arms, murmuring, 'I love you, Amy, but promise me you'll think long and hard about all this.'

'Yes,' she said.

'When you have decided, call me. I won't see you again until then, it will give you time and space to think.'

They clung to each other as if about to be shipwrecked.

'Now, now,' he scolded 'We must be strong.' He glanced over his shoulder. 'Let's have our coffee and then I should go.'

When the door closed behind him, she breathed deeply as if she had been running. Giorgio! He came to mind and she realised that in these past feverish hours she had given him no thought. Giorgio, devoted to her, believing they might have a future together. She must also decide what she would say to him. Amy was surprised to find herself praying: God give me strength.

Her first instinct was to turn to Paolo for advice. But Davide had sworn her to secrecy. 'The fewer people who know what I do the better,' he'd said. This was a choice she must make alone. She sank down on the sofa, too tired to dress and face the world.

Two days later when she forced herself to go back to her market stall, she brushed off Matilde and Salvatore's concern, well aware that she sounded brusque. Her mind was elsewhere as she set out her spices and greeted her first customers with a wan smile. Giorgio's voice startled her and she gazed at him as if he were a stranger.

'I've been trying to get hold of you,' he explained. 'Is your phone out of order?'

'Yes.' She had left it off the hook.

'I've been wondering whether Carlo being my cousin might have spoiled things between us. The police have been to see him about another matter.'

She thought of the strange marks on his arm

'He has hepatitis, Amy.' He sighed. 'It's better you hear it from me: he's a drug user.'

The Largo Argentina vet had spoken of complications following cat scratches. 'So he's quite ill?'

'A fever and swollen lymph glands, they've got him on antibiotics. I only hope he hasn't been dealing. He'll go down for some time, if he has.'

'He deserves to suffer, Giorgio. He's a monster.'

He pressed his lips together, seeming to be at a loss as to what to say.

'A monster!' she repeated. 'A murderer!'

The tension between them grew until he spoke at last. 'Yes, he has done wrong, time and again, but Amy, he's family.'

Without meeting his eye, she muttered: 'Oh yes, family. Why am I not surprised?'

'There's something else wrong,' he persisted. 'You're not your usual self.'

The understatement might have made her smile. Instead she felt angry with him. She said: 'Well you might not have been the one to kill those cats, but you don't like them, do you?'

He sighed. 'Oh Amy, don't bring all that up again. You know my reasons, I've tried to explain to you. It never meant I wanted to harm them.'

She knew she was being unfair but, filled with guilt, she pushed on. 'And at your father's birthday party you stopped me talking about them.'

'Maybe I overreacted. It is just Maria can be a little extreme in her views. I didn't want to spoil Dad's birthday.'

Amy muttered 'Family, family, family! That's all you Italians think about!' She made a business of rearranging some packages of spices, not wishing to see his hurt expression.

'You're behaving very strangely. I don't know what's got into you.'

She made no answer.

'You seem different, Amy.'

When she still didn't reply, a range of emotions seemed to cross his face –hurt, confusion and anger. Then he sighed. 'Oh well, I'll leave you alone until you're in a better mood.' he turned and walked away.

Amy stared after Giorgio as all the pent-up emotion overwhelmed her. She'd never intended to deal with the situation in such a clumsy way. What had come over her? She sank down onto her chair, sobbing. In a trice Matilde and Salvatore were by her side. But to their questions as to what was wrong she could give no answer.

'It will be better tomorrow,' Salvatore suggested.

Matilde was more perceptive and suggested she get away for a few days. It dawned on Amy that this was a good idea, but where? Then she remembered that, on more than one occasion, Paolo had offered her his apartment in Menton.

******

'I need to get away,' she told him when they met for a drink the following evening. She'd found her return to the empty apartment unbearable.

'Is there something wrong?' he queried. 'Forgive me, but you don't look as if you've slept very well.'

She was tempted to tell him the truth, confident that he would keep it to himself. But if there was the slightest risk of putting Davide in danger she knew she must stay silent.

''I'm facing a tricky situation,' she said. 'But I'll tell you one thing: Davide has made things clear.'

'I see.'

'No, it's not what you think.' She was on the brink of continuing but stopped herself. 'I can't say anything more.'

'Then don't. I understand'.

'Do you?' she was half inclined to believe he did. Paolo had always shown impressive insight when it came to things of the heart. Sometimes she felt he could read her mind.

'Make your arrangements,' he was saying. 'I'll drop the Menton apartment keys off to you tomorrow.'

The next day passed in a flurry of activity as she checked timetables, booked tickets and packed a case. Susan at the sanctuary had to be alerted of her absence and surprised Amy by saying she was relieved to see her taking a break. 'Have I been looking that awful?' she joked.

'I just think you need some space,' Susan said.

XXXIX

As the time of her train's departure approached and she was preparing to leave she was overwhelmed by a sense of nostalgia. She took a last look round the apartment as if on her return things would never be the same. On the train, the guard came to prepare her couchette and by nine she had climbed into it feeling exhausted. But the disembodied voices announcing the various stations, the shunting of the train from one track to another disturbed her sleep and echoed in her dreams. At Ventimiglia she changed trains having been warned by Paolo to get out at the Menton Garavan stop where his friend Francois would be waiting.

'He'll help you with your case to the apartment, it is a little distance away.'

Amy had been curious to meet Paolo's reason for his frequent trips to Menton. She was not sure quite what she expected. Certainly someone of roughly the same age, not this slim, dark bearded man who must be scarcely in his forties.

'Mademoiselle Armstrong, delighted to meet you.' He shook her hand. To her relief he spoke English, if with a strong accent. 'Did you have a good journey?'

'Yes,' she lied but she could not help reflecting his charming smile. You old dog, Paolo, she thought. No wonder you always look so good after one of your trips.

Francois seized her case. `Shall we go?'

He led the way to a rather battered looking Citroen parked in the station precinct. 'Excuse the state of my car, but I was up in the mountains for a festival yesterday and home rather late.'

Seated beside him, the lemony scent of his cologne was familiar, it was one Paolo used. Amy remembered that Menton was famous for its lemons and imagined them shopping together in some exclusive perfumery. She was seeing another side to her friend.

François put his foot on the accelerator and they shot out of the precinct.

She caught a glimpse of very blue sea, bright sunshine, and a long promenade thronging with people, and then they took a right upward turn. They passed several Belle Epoque buildings and came to a halt outside one no less grand than the others.

'Here?' she asked.

Francois laughed. 'Not all of it, just the ground floor apartment.'

It was, as she expected, beautifully furnished, Louis Quatorze pieces set off by some of a more modern style. Francois showed her the bedroom with its draped muslin curtains and large bed, a pretty kitchen where a percolator stood side by side with a kettle (in case being English you might prefer tea, he said.) Flowers and a bowl of fruit welcomed her. But it was the terrace that held her attention with its small iron table and two chairs surrounded by palms and ferns.

'I don't think I'll stir from here,' she said.

'Ah, but then you would miss the promenade by the sea and the magnificent Botanical garden.'

'We'll see.'

'Do as you wish. You will find tranquillity here. There is my number by the telephone. Call me if you need anything, anything at all.'

With that he left her. She found a bottle of wine in the fridge, which had also been stocked with food. She went to sit on the terrace and let the peace of the place wash over her. Silently she thanked Paolo who had given her this respite.

Later, curiosity got the better of her and she walked down the road to the promenade. It was a balmy evening and there were still a few bathers in the sea. A heat haze merged water with sky. She found an empty bench and sat there watching people pass to and fro, children begging ice cream, elderly men and women, couples… how she envied them, they seemed without a care in the world.

The following day, after an excellent night's sleep she walked into the town to explore the market. She bought cherries scooped from a glistening dark mound and tiny wild strawberries nestled in tissue paper. A stallholder urged her to look at her flowers and persuaded Amy to buy a bouquet of roses and baby's breath. She drank *café*

au lait in a nearby café and found herself imagining she
lived here. The pace of life seemed much slower than
Rome and no one knew her whereabouts but Paolo. By
the end of the next day she was feeling sufficiently
relaxed to ask herself whether she wanted to resume all
the complexities of Davide, or for that matter Giorgio.
She seemed to have been lulled into a trance-like state
composed of sun and blue skies where nothing else
mattered but eating, sleeping and going for long strolls by
the sea. She became aware that she was letting go of
months of scarcely interrupted work, shedding anxieties
and sorrows, and reaching into the core of herself. Apart
from the market stallholders, she spoke to no one and no
one spoke to her. In this way, several pleasant days
passed. Amy savoured every moment, aware this couldn't
last. Sooner or later she would have to face up to reality
and return to Rome. 'Not quite yet,' she found herself
murmuring as she sat on the terrace with her coffee,
watching yet another day bloom around her. There was a
small bird that seemed particularly tame and she had
taken to throwing it crumbs from her morning croissants.
Time seemed distilled in these small pleasures and she
was content until there came one early morning when she
woke with tears streaming down her face. In her dream
Davide was standing before the mirror in the apartment.
He had his back to her but she could see his reflection in
the glass as he spoke. 'I understand you want nothing
more to do with me,' he was saying. 'It's only fair, you
have your life to lead.'

She woke, shouting: 'No that's not what I want,' She got up and went out onto the terrace to sit there until dawn broke. But this dawn was different. The ease of the last few days had vanished. She went for a stroll on the promenade, sat to watch the people passing but now she felt apart, a stranger. It couldn't have lasted, she thought, gazing out to sea, at the happy bathers, I'm just a visitor, I don't belong here. Tomorrow she would call Francois to thank him and say she was leaving. With her decision made, she would return to Rome.

Almost to her surprise, the apartment looked exactly the same as when she'd left it, as if it had been waiting for her. With a sigh of relief she dropped her bag and went into the kitchen to make a mug of coffee. Then not daring to leave it until her resolve had deserted her, she dialled Giorgio's number.

XL

His mother answered. 'I'm sorry Amy, he's away on a dig.'

'Oh dear, when will he be back?'

'I really don't know.' Chrissie's tone was cool. 'He just said he'd be away for some time.'

Amy was feeling uncomfortable. She needed to say what she had to say but it wasn't something that could be done over the phone. 'Do you think I could come to see you then?' she heard pleading in her tone.

'Oh Amy, do you think that's a good idea? Surely it's Giorgio…'

'Please Chrissie, just for a while.'

There came an audible sigh before Chrissie spoke. 'OK, tomorrow around one, come for a bite of lunch. Can you make it then?'

As the tram took her to the Pigneto district, she couldn't help but compare this trip with the last time when she and Giorgio travelled there together. His father's birthday party had seemed to mark a turning point in their relationship. The welcome she'd received from the family set her imagination working as to how life might be if she married Giorgio: comfortable, secure with probably two or three children. All would be transparent, out in the open. She'd realised she was becoming tired of uncertainty. That was before Davide made his sudden re-appearance.

In Pigneto, she wandered aimlessly in the crowded market and had to ask the way. Finally, she found herself in front of the house with the lemon trees in the front garden. Chrissie answered the door so promptly Amy felt she must have been loitering in the hall. Perhaps she was just as apprehensive. Dressed, as before in dungarees, her hair in a ponytail, her manner was cool. She led the way to the kitchen where a table was set. 'Hope you don't mind but we're eating in here today as it's just me and you.'

Amy shook her head. Lunch was the last thing on her mind. Chrissie ladled out bowls of soup and sat down.

'I suppose you've come about Carlo? To be honest it wasn't a huge surprise, he's a very unpleasant character and I had my suspicions about his drug taking. You don't work with these kids without knowing something about it. I'm glad he's been caught even if he is part of my husband's family, which means they'll close ranks and attempt to defend him. Those poor kitties.'

Amy took up her spoon, laid it down again. 'No, it's not Carlo. I'd like to talk to you about Giorgio.'

'Ah, Giorgio.'

There was a pause. Amy nervously crumbled bread. 'Has he said anything to you?' she asked, at last.

'Not as such, but I know my son. I guessed there was something wrong when he suddenly said he had to get away.'

The soup forgotten, Chrissie met Amy's gaze who was surprised to see a new gentleness in the woman's eyes. She had expected a mother's anger.

'He loves you, Amy but I don't think you feel the same way. Am I right? Oh don't look so surprised! I guessed it at that birthday party. It was then I began to worry that Giorgio might get hurt.'

At this Amy felt a great weight of guilt but seized the opening. She nodded. 'Yes, you are right. It isn't that I don't respect and admire your son, I do and I am very fond of him. At one point, I thought we could make a go of it…' she tailed off.

Impulsively Chrissie rose and brought a bottle of wine to the table. She filled their glasses and took a sip. 'But, there is a but, isn't there?'

This is what she needed to say, nevertheless when the opportunity came, it wasn't easy. Amy spoke quietly: 'I'm in love with someone else.'

'I suspected it. One can't help one's feelings, Amy. We can fight them, sure, but they have a way of winning.' Chrissie gave her a quick smile and clinked their glasses. She raised hers in salute, the atmosphere tangibly lightening.

'I'm glad you've been honest,' she said. 'Far better now than to go on pretending.'

'I hate to hurt Giorgio.'

'He'll suffer, we all have to, unless we're lucky.' Chrissie seemed to consider this. 'Although maybe we grow with these experiences, we finally step into the shoes of the person we are meant to be.'

Amy said: 'that doesn't stop me feeling guilty.'

'I expect you do, you're a lovely person, Amy. I wouldn't expect anything else. But Giorgio's young, he'll get over it.'

They drank their wine and Chrissie brought cheese and crackers to the table. A closeness that hadn't existed before developed between them. Amy felt a twinge of regret that she and Chrissie would probably never meet again. She wondered if she would have the same sympathetic reception from Davide's mother, or would the woman view her as an outsider as *Signora* Giordano had her mother? She was about to ask Chrissie how she had coped with marrying an Italian when the other, glancing at her watch, said it was time she headed back to work. They said goodbye and embraced.

Amy took a last glance round the apartment. If she saw Giorgio again it would not be here. She wondered whether he would contact her.

Outside once more she paused, took a deep breath and stepped out towards the tram stop. As it trundled back to the centre she felt a sense of relief. She had taken the first step. The way forward looked clearer.

XLI

'I hope the cats will be alright.' Giulia said. 'We've never left them so long together before.'

They were on their way to Trastevere where a former colleague of Gian Franco had invited them to his granddaughter's christening. Giulia had returned late from the hairdresser and then spent a good half hour agonising over the outfit she'd chosen. For once it was Gian Franco who had to urge her to get a move on. It was Saturday and several times their taxi was held up by traffic. The garden of St Michael's already thronged with guests when they arrived. Under the July sun, the faces of the men in suits were shiny with sweat. In contrast, their wives, wearing light, summery dresses, looked comfortable and cool.

'Oh, see how stylish they are,' Giulia muttered. 'I wish I hadn't listened to you and bought something new.'

'Don't be silly, you look fine.'

She wanted to look far more than just fine. 'Chic, stylish, well dressed were the words she wanted to hear. Fine! What he really meant was she just looked okay.

Gian Franco took her arm to urge her forward. It wasn't like Giulia to feel inferior. Father Bruno stood at the church door ready to welcome the congregation. The baby, star of the day, arrived in the arms of his mother, dressed in an elaborate white gown sewn with pearls. On his head a round cap also featured pearls. When he had been sufficiently cooed over, people filed inside.

Seated at the back of the church, Giulia began a whispered commentary on the status quo of the various guests.

'That's Anna Maria, she was married to Vincenzo. what was his name? But she's with someone different today. How young he is! What happened to Elena Cassone's husband, do you know? Did he die? Is that Margerita Soldano? My God, she's aged.'

Gian Franco was grateful when the service began.

Father Bruno went to town on this christening. He had chosen as his subject the experience of being a godparent or a godchild.

'Well done to all those of you who have recently become godparents, including the *padrino* of little Francesco Piero today. You are setting out on a great and privileged role. Pour out your love and care and prayers on your godchild. Help them to journey in Christian faith. Rejoice and give thanks that you have been asked to serve in this way. Perhaps seek the help of others here as you fulfil that wonderful role which God has given you.'

As the sermon continued, Gian Franco felt himself nodding off to be sharply awakened by Giulia's elbow digging him in the ribs. He glanced at his watch and sighed.

Having described memories of his own godfather and more recent joys as godfather to nephews and nieces,

Father Bruno gave a surreptitious glance at his watch and brought his sermon to its end. 'Love and care, prayer, being there, being the bearer of the message "the Kingdom of God is near", encouraging the journey of Christian faith – all these fall within the calling and vocation of a godparent – and all these can bring great blessing to a godchild.'

The choir's Ave Maria filled the church, the congregation rose and filed out into the sunshine.

'Will you come to the reception?' they heard the newly christened baby's mother ask the priest.

'I'd love to but I have another christening after his one.'

Giulia sidled over to him. 'Come after that, Father, do. I shall be so disappointed if you don't.'

He smiled. 'How can I refuse?'

A spread greeted them when they arrived in the garden of the hotel where the reception took place. The setting was dominated by a three-tiered cake with baby blue icing, which Gian Franco found rather daunting. There were prawn vol au vents, mini pizzas and tiny sandwiches. Gian Franco made a beeline for the huge Baci chocolates stuffed with ice cream. Paper flower bouquets and balloons decorated the garden and champagne loosened people's tongues. A woman in a low cut dress splodged with huge pink roses introduced herself to Gian Franco as Lucia, the best friend of the baby's grandmother. She seemed to assume she had known him from his library days, although he couldn't place her.

'You've weathered well, I have to say,' she told him. 'You don't look that much different to the handsome young man who helped me choose books.'

Gian Franco preened. Across the table, Giulia caught sight of them laughing together and, when the woman touched her husband's arm, she realised she felt jealous.

She arrived at his side. 'Pardon me but I wanted to remind my husband it's time to give the baby his gift.'

Flustered he felt in his pockets and brought out a gold angel pendant. Giulia pounced on it and wrapped it in a scrap of tissue paper.

'Husbands,' murmured Lucia in an attempt at female solidarity.

Giulia ignored her. 'Are you coming, Gian Franco?'

A crowd had gathered round the baby's parents as they accepted the gifts. In return they handed out the *bomboniera*, each little box containing a glass swan, topped with five sugared almonds wrapped in tulle. At that point Francesco Piero decided he'd had enough and began to cry. Not long after he was borne away, and soon the party began to break up.

In the taxi going home, Giulia was thoughtful. 'I'm sorry we never had any children,' she said at last. 'I know you wanted them.'

For a moment they dwelt on the several miscarriages they had grieved together.

Gian Franco gave her hand a reassuring squeeze. 'It just wasn't meant to be.'

'No, but…'

'Tesoro, you are enough for me.' He laughed. 'More than enough, sometimes!'

Giulia felt a sense of unity hardly ever expressed before. All those years and they were still together. 'You're a good man, Gian Franco,' she said. 'I love you.'

He reached over and kissed her. 'And I love you. Now let's go and see what those cats have been up to.'

XLII

Amy felt overcome by the enormity of what she was about to do. She stood by the window, staring down at the square without really seeing it. 'Calm yourself, Amy,' she spoke aloud. But the thought of what would lie ahead made her heart beat fast.

She took several deep breaths and went to lift the telephone receiver and dial Davide's number. But there was no answer. Perhaps in her nervous state she had dialled the wrong number. She tried again, imagining it ringing in the apartment she had never visited. An empty apartment? Fear washed over her. Surely Davide couldn't run out on her again. Had he taken her prolonged silence as a refusal and already left Rome? She managed a brief message and hung up. Her eyes brimmed with tears, blurring familiar objects as she gazed round as if seeking answers. 'Oh Davide,' she murmured. 'If you'd only waited.' The shrill of the telephone made her start.

Davide's voice quickened her heart. 'Amy I'm so sorry. I was at the café when you called. What's the matter, darling?' he continued as her tears started in earnest.

'Nothing.' She sniffed. 'I'm just so relieved to hear your voice.'

'You thought…?'

'Yes.'

'Oh tesoro, I promised.'

She scrabbled for a tissue, blew her nose and missed his next words.

'So you've decided?' he repeated.

She hesitated but only for a moment. 'Yes Davide, I have. I want to be with you.'

She heard an intake of breath. 'I'm very happy,' he said. 'But only if you are absolutely sure.'

Amy was smiling now 'Absolutely.'

'You'll take me on with all that it involves?'

'I will.'

There was a pause and then Davide said: 'Enough to say you'll marry me?'

Her smile stretched to a broad grin. 'Yes, Davide, oh yes. Of course I will.'

******

'Well, this is a surprise to say the least,' her mother said. 'I don't know what to say. You've never mentioned there was anyone special in your life.'

'I'm sorry Mum but it's all been rather complicated.'

'Complicated? That sounds intriguing. What's his name?'

'Davide.' Amy smiled to herself. She was going to marry him and she still didn't know his surname.

'Ah, an Italian, how did you meet him?'

The tone of her voice made Amy hesitate before answering. 'He rescued me from a pickpocketing gypsy.'

She heard the familiar click of a lighter as her mother started on yet another cigarette. She was obviously trying to take this in. 'And it just developed from there?'

'Not exactly, Mum. He has a very demanding job that takes him away often.'

'Oh.' Her mother was becoming intrigued. 'So what does he do?'

'He's a policeman.'

'A policeman!' Caroline gave a short barking laugh. 'Amy really! The majority of policemen I came across in Rome spent their time lounging on street corners and eyeing up girls.'

'Not that kind of policeman.' Could she trust her mother? Amy took a deep breath and lowered her voice. 'He belongs to the Catturandi.'

'The what?'

'Oh Mum, it's a special branch. I'm not saying anymore.'

'Someone quite high up, then, well that puts a different perspective on things. There'll be a big wedding, I suppose.'

At this point Amy didn't have the heart to tell her that there'd be no such ceremony. Davide had told her that it would have to be a quiet, intimate affair with two witnesses. She could imagine her mother was already starting to make plans and hesitated to disenchant her.

She still found it hard to believe that she and Davide would be together to face whatever danger threatened.

'I'll let you know when our plans are a bit more forward.'

'Do give us plenty of warning,' her mother urged. 'I'll need to organise the shop and your father will want to give you something nice for a wedding present.' She paused, inhaled. 'Darling, are you really sure about this?'

'I couldn't be more sure, Mum. I love him with all my heart.'

'Then I'm happy for you, Amy.'

XLIII

The second christening of the day had been a difficult affair. The baby had screamed and almost wriggled out of his arms as he sprinkled water from the font. The child's mother had let out a scream and accused the priest of clumsiness. The family had departed leaving behind a litter of sweet papers. Father Bruno felt exhausted and decided not to accept the invitation to join the celebration for baby Francesco Piero after all.

The following morning he returned to find that little had been done to clean, or remove yesterday's flowers, which surprised him, as *Signora* Mancini was usually so punctilious. As he entered the church he was struck by an almost preternatural silence. He walked towards the altar and was stopped short in his tracks. His cleaner sat slumped in one of the pews. It was as he had anticipated, the work had become too much for her and she had collapsed. It was his duty to tell her now she must retire. He advanced closer to touch her gently on the shoulder then drew his hand away. He peered closer. *Signora* Mancini was dead. God in heaven, if only he had realised, she must have been more ill than anyone knew. Father Bruno stood for a moment gazing down at her, noting the work-worn hands where the wedding ring hung loose on her finger. He thought of the years of service this woman had given to St Michael's, her enduring faith and devotion to his church. He remembered how protective she had been of him on the day when the cat murderer had left him so shaken. He would miss her dearly. A ray of sun burst through the coloured glass of the window and seemed to illuminate her as his lips moved in the prayers of absolution: 'Forgive whatever sins she committed through human weakness and in your goodness grant her eternal rest.' Then he thanked God that she had died in the place she loved.

Later when the ambulance had come to take *Signora* Mancini's body away, he returned to his house and called Father Eustachio. In the other priest's study they opened a bottle of vino Santo and drank to the dead woman. He related the light that had seemed to surround her, as he'd prayed, transforming her expression into one of perfect peace. He remarked how extraordinary it had seemed as if an angel had taken her away.

Father Eustachio, not so convinced about the passage of angels, conceded that God moved in mysterious ways.

'She was a lesson to us all,' Father Bruno mused. 'A simple woman in the truest sense who lived to serve others, as our Lord taught us.'

Eustachio nodded, cursing himself for the logic that at times continued to plague him and cause the detachment that his friend obviously didn't feel. It was all very well wanting to serve others, but not at the cost of her health and her very life. The conversation turned to the funeral that, Bruno said, would naturally be conducted at St Michael's.

Father Eustachio was unprepared for the occurrence that happened in the middle of the night when he was awoken by a voice saying: 'Eustachio you are chosen, do not fight but come to Me. I will shelter you with my wings. I will be your Saviour.'

XLIV

It felt strange to climb down the metal steps to the cat sanctuary once more. Only a few days had passed, but it seemed to Amy she'd been away much longer. Her first thought was to look for Shadow and to her delight he came running when she called. She sank on her haunches to stroke him and as he arched his back in pleasure she could feel a deep rumbling purr. 'I'm sorry I've been away but something wonderful has happened.' She buried her face in his soft grey fur. 'Have you missed me?' She gazed into his amber eyes. He seemed to listen in silence, and reassure with his frank, non-judgmental gaze that in all this there was a design, if she could but perceive it. She thought of that April day when she had seen him for the first time and been drawn here. Life seemed to have come full circle and now she felt grateful to fate that had brought her to this moment.

'He certainly has missed you.' Susan had come to stand over her. 'We all have, sweetie. How was your break? It looks as if it's done you good.'

She was on the verge of telling Susan her news but checked herself, wondering whether she should.

'Menton was lovely,' she said instead.

'Isn't it? I spent a vacation there, a couple of years ago. I loved the Botanical Gardens. Did you go there?'

Not wishing to admit how little she had done, Amy nodded and changed the subject. 'What's new?'

'Well, this man, Carlo Bevacqua is quite ill with cat scratch fever. I don't know if you know this but the police have questioned him and it seems he is involved in drug dealing. It's likely he'll go to prison.' Susan gave a loud sniff. ''Unless they go soft and offer therapy. Therapy! In my opinion anyone who does what he did is just plain evil and deserves all he gets.'

'I agree, only a sadist could inflict such pain.'

'It's cast a shadow over the whole family, of course. Didn't you hang out with one of them at some point?'

Hang out was hardly the term, Amy thought with a pang, if you're talking about the man I considered marrying.

Memories of another pain were revived when Susan showed her the rescued kittens that had been found in a rubbish bag and were now growing fast. Amy watched as they played and tangled with each other. They seemed so full of life. An image of the little creature that had died in her arms still brought a lump to her throat.

'We've found lovely homes for them to go to,' the American woman sounded proud. 'Our latest adoption drive has done very well.'

Amy listened with a sense of detachment. Her forthcoming wedding seemed to have occupied her mind to such a degree she found it hard to concentrate on anything else. When they were married she could return here in a more tranquil state of mind. She had no intention of relinquishing any of her former life here in Rome, she had struggled to attain her independence and she knew Davide would understand. Perhaps they could even adopt a cat. It would depend on where they chose to live. She hoped it would be Rome.

Before she could broach the subject with Davide, he told her there was something else he had to say. 'I should have mentioned it before but I've been putting it off. I was afraid it might make you change your mind.'

The old sense of insecurity crept back. What now?

They'd driven upward to the Aventine Hill to gaze out over the city. Amy remembered the first time they'd been there at the very beginning of their relationship. Couples had stood hand in hand to watch the sunset and she'd longed for Davide to kiss her. Now as they found a bench and sat with his arm around her, he said: 'don't look so alarmed! I'm not going to die on you, silly.' His expression did nothing to reassure her. He turned away for a moment, gazing out at the sky. She waited. He sighed.

'Then Davide, what is it? Please tell me.'

He turned back to meet her gaze. 'I'm sorry, my darling, but I'm afraid we can't have children. Since Falcone's assassination the Mafia is nervous and trigger happy, they are out to get anyone who opposes them. If anything happened to us, where would those children be?'

Amy was silent, absorbing this. With the exhilaration of Davide's proposal she had not, until this moment, given children any thought. Now it struck her with surprising force and she realised she had taken for granted they would have children. She was marrying an Italian, after all, and living in a country where family was everything. An image of a child with Davide's eyes flitted into her mind. Their new home might have had a garden where he could play. She saw herself pushing a swing with a delighted child crying 'higher'. But was this yet another aspect of the reality she would be taking on in marrying a special policeman?

'It makes me sad to say this as there is nothing I'd like more,' Davide looked anxious, 'but what about you, darling?'

The image lingered a moment longer, the feel of small arms round her neck, the scent of his baby skin, one she had never envisaged until this moment when it was not to be. Davide was right, of course, she couldn't deny it but...

'Amy?'

She realised he was watching her, fearful of her reaction. She banished the image and reached out to stroke his face. 'If that is the deal for being with you then so be it.'

She saw him relax. 'I was so nervous to say this but I am glad you understand.'

He pulled her to him and she nestled in the warmth of his body and knew, in spite of any sacrifice, she didn't want to be anywhere else.

XLV

She was thrown into confusion, however, when a few days later, Giorgio rang and asked to see her. His voice was calm, without a trace of anger. They arranged to meet. He was standing in the shadow of the Santa Maria church in Piazza del Popolo and for a moment she gazed at him unseen. She felt a sharp pang of regret looking back over the past months and the times they had spent together. Whatever his mother had said, she did feel guilty. Maybe with time his bruised feelings would mend but today, taken unawares, she could see raw emotion in his expression. The next moment he caught sight of her and, putting on a smile, started forward.

'Amy I'm glad to see you. Shall we go and sit over there?'

With a heavy heart she followed him to the cafe table set a little apart from the others. They sat gazing out over the wide square and she sensed the contrast of their silence with the happy chatter going on around them. She hardly noticed Giorgio order until the waiter set two glasses of Cinzano on their table and added a bowl of olives. After the ease of their many conversations, neither appeared to know what to say and certainly not how to broach the subject both knew they were here for. It was also obvious they were reluctant to mention Carlo.

Giorgio set down his glass. 'So how was your day?'

She shrugged. 'Oh, you know, the usual.'

'Have you come up with any more of your weird and wonderful recipes?"

This was awful.

'No,' she said. 'Not really.'

They lapsed into silence again.

Giorgio cleared his throat. 'We found another cache of stolen artefacts yesterday. I spent all day cataloguing them.'

'Oh, that's good.' Her throat was constricted, incapable of speech. She felt she might cry.

He seemed to sense this and reached out to take her hand. 'Don't upset yourself, Amy, I understand.'

She looked up then and met his gaze, the dark eyes gentle with love and concern. It was too much to bear.

'Oh Giorgio, I'm so sorry.'

He managed a wry smile turning it into a joke. 'And so you should be!' No really,' he continued, 'I think I've known all along but I tried to ignore it. Your heart has never been truly with me.'

This was worse than the reproach she had expected.

'I wanted to believe it could be, and I almost did,' she murmured. 'You're a dear sweet man and I knew I could be happy with you only…'

'Only Davide came back on the scene.' A note of bitterness crept into his voice. 'The man who could vanish for months without a word.'

How could she explain this sense that something had been missing from her life and always would be without Davide?

'I didn't choose this passion, Giorgio, it chose me, that might sound dramatic but it's true. I kept trying to convince myself that following my heart would be a difficult path but now it's the one I know I have to take.' A tear ran down her cheek.

People's voices and laughter washed over them. Giorgio stared at her as though searching for something to say. Then he stirred himself. 'That reminds me, I have a little gift for you.' He reached in his pocket and brought out a small long necked glass bottle.

Amy, turning it over in her hands, noted the ancient patina then looked up at him enquiringly.

'It's a Roman tear bottle. It is said that when someone died the bereaved collected their tears. When the tears had evaporated, the mourning period was over.'

Watching his face she was struck by the sudden realisation that over these past months she had come to love Giorgio, perhaps not with the passion she had for Davide but with a sense of security and contentment. Her future might have lacked drama but would have been steady and devoted to family life. She might have had his children. She realised a part of her still harboured disappointment that with Davide this would never be. Amy reached over and kissed him on the cheek. She had hurt him and she didn't know how to assuage it 'Thank you,' was all she could manage.

He pushed back his chair and rose to his feet as if he must escape. 'But I hope there won't be many tears in your new life,' he said. 'Use it for perfume instead.'

XLVI

Father Eustachio recognised the girl at once. She was the nice little *gattara*, Amy, from Largo Argentina who had talked to him about the cat poisoner. Thankfully the man had been caught although not, he understood, by the efforts of Bruno and his dubious security camera. His fellow priest had been disappointed by the blurriness of the intruder's images. However, the statue of St. Gertrude was saved from further besmirching.

But who was the good looking young man with her? As the priest entered the church he saw them standing in front of the statue. Amy appeared to be recounting something to him. Whatever it was the young man looked totally absorbed by her. Eustachio felt his heart melt at the sight.

******

She was relating the experience she had had in the Borghese gardens, last autumn. 'It was very strange. I was on the point of leaving Rome, as there didn't seem much point in staying any longer. I'd heard nothing from you for so long and I felt that my time here had come to an end. It was raining and I turned back from my walk along one of those avenues. It was then I saw the bench, which had been empty a moment before, was occupied.'

Afterwards she had queried whether what she saw had been in her imagination or, in fact a vision. The woman who sat there with a cat on her lap had looked curiously like the saint. 'Their gaze had seemed to inspire me to hang on here. After a moment I walked on and when I looked back, they'd disappeared. You don't believe me, do you, Davide?' she finished.

'My dearest Amy, if you told me the moon was made of blue cheese, of course I'd believe you.'

Laughing she shook her head. 'You don't!'

Davide caught sight of Father Eustachio. 'Ah just the person we want to see.'

They sat in the priest's study to discuss their plans. Though neither went regularly to church they said nothing of this, only that their faiths were different.

'As Amy is Protestant and I Catholic we thought we'd have a civil ceremony and then a church blessing, if that is possible?'

Father Eustachio watched the young man as he spoke, the way he referred constantly to Amy and she to him. Already they seemed to him belonging to each other in what he could only describe as a spiritual way. This is true love, he thought, an echo of the divine when God's gift of love courses through both of you and radiates to others. He felt joyful in their presence.

'That can be arranged,' he said. 'Have you set a date?'

They smiled at each other and the young man took Amy's hand. 'As soon as possible,' he said.

'I keep thinking I'll wake up and this will all be a dream,' Amy said as they came out into the sunshine once more.

Davide took her arm. 'It's real all right, my darling. Come on, the day's not over yet. We have some shopping to do.'

Puzzled, she allowed herself to be led into the heart of the historic centre. Davide seemed to know exactly where he was heading, turning into ever-smaller streets until he halted her in front of a jeweller's shop.

'We must choose an engagement ring, tesoro.'

The elderly jeweller brought a tray of rings, each sparkling in the light of the overhead chandelier. Amy felt dazzled by their beauty, bewildered in making a choice.

'I've never done this before,' she appealed to the jeweller.

Both men laughed.

'I should hope not!' Davide said in mock horror. 'Nor ever again.'

She returned to gaze at the rings. Should it be this one? That one? 'What do you think, Davide?'

'Well, this one with the amethyst is pretty.'

'Oh yes, or the green stone? I don't know what it is.'

They met each other's gaze and she saw the occasion was an emotional one for him, too and the choice extremely important.

The jeweller seemed to sense this and came to the rescue. 'If I may make a suggestion, which month is the young lady's birthday?'

'September.' They spoke in unison.

'Ah then how about a ring with your birthstone? A sapphire?'

Amy stared at the ring he indicated: a dazzling oval sapphire surrounded by small diamonds, the setting and band of white gold.

'Magnificent!' Davide's voice came to her as she continued to gaze.

It was certainly stunning and seemed to her now as the only one to choose. She felt overcome by the enormity of this occasion.

'You like it, Amy?' Davide asked.

She couldn't speak, just nodded.

'Then we'll have it, please.'

'You've chosen well,' the elderly man said. 'It is a classic ring.' He lifted it out and was about to put it in a small box but Davide stopped him. Taking hold of Amy's hand, he slipped it on her finger. It fitted perfectly. They embraced.

The jeweller said: 'Congratulations.' His voice was husky with emotion.

That evening, Davide took her to *Grappolo D'Oro* and ordered champagne. The sapphire glittered on her finger and Amy could not stop looking at it.

Davide raised his glass to her. 'By the way, I've found the perfect place for our wedding, the lakeside at Bracciano. Remember, I promised you we'd go back there.'

Tears came to her eyes. 'Oh Davide, I never dreamed it would be for this.'

He patted her hand. 'Sweetheart, don't cry. This is a happy occasion.'

'I know,' she sniffed. 'And I'm just so happy!'

They laughed and kissed and the other diners, guessing this was a special occasion, burst into applause.

XLVII

September arrived, Amy's second in Rome and the month of her birthday. The intense heat of summer gave way to comfortable warmth by day, and crisp evenings with the hint of autumn just around the corner. At Largo Argentina, volunteers gave a sigh of relief. Unlike the cats, their lot during baking July and August was not to snooze away the day in the shade of the ruins.

Other kinds of fruit and vegetables appeared on Matilde's market stall, a further sign of the transition of the seasons. Gone were the strawberries and apricots, the artichoke and green fava beans. In their place there were nutty and earthy porcini mushrooms, apples, peaches and pumpkins. Figs, the sweet green second harvest, were ready to yield their syrupy flavour.

For once, the stallholder lost her sharp tongue and was all smiles, exalting September. 'It's my favourite month, ah, how I love it. On Sunday we do the *vendemmia*, eh Salvatore? The grapes are beautiful this year. Mother Nature has been kind with the weather, no hailstorms and no rain. *Grazie a Dio*. Listen Amy, in a few weeks' time I'll take you out to my family's land and we'll collect wild greens, oh and mushrooms, of course. Salvie, you can come too, if you behave yourself.'

******

It had rained for two days but on the day of the outing a perfect September day bloomed into clear blue skies after the early mist had cleared. Amy and Davide followed the others' cars leaving Rome for the countryside. For once Davide had forgone his usual careful dressing and wore old jeans and a tee shirt.

'Street urchin,' Amy teased him, echoing his description of her all those months ago.

'I could say the same of you,' he laughed. 'But you look lovely in anything.' He gave her a quick kiss.

'Now then, you two lovebirds,' Matilde called to them, 'we have work to do. You're going to have to earn the feast I've made for you.'

Salvatore made them all stand in a circle round him while he ran through his 'rules'. 'Don't pick the very small mushrooms. If you don't allow them to reach a reasonable size they will not have released their spores. Use your knife to cut the mushroom at the base. Don't just rip it out or you will damage the underground part.'

Armed with wicker baskets they set out among the trees. The undergrowth was warm and damp and mushrooms were pushing up through the wet grasses. The air was chill, fresh and lovely. When the sun broke through, the dying bracken blazed and then it was all golden and beautiful on this autumn morning. Eyes firmly fixed on its floor they followed trails specified by Salvatore, who had appointed himself the mushroom expert. It was not long before the silence was broken by the shrieks of a happy picker. Soon everyone was absorbed, walking quietly, staring at the ground, then pouncing with glee. Chanterelles blended into the autumn bracken; spy one and suddenly a dozen more came into focus. Hedgehog mushrooms flashed white at the foot of trees, identified by the spines underneath. Now and again, someone would run back to Salvatore to check the safety of a particular fungus.

'No, you can't eat that one, throw it away. No, that's a sulphur cap not a cow bolete. It wouldn't kill you but it's not nice to eat. Yes, that's a chanterelle, you can tell it by the dimple on top. Wonderful chanterelles,' he commented.

There came the sound of rain pitter-pattering on the canopy of leaves above their heads. But Salvatore was jubilant. 'Good weather for mushrooms,' he crowed. They used wicker baskets for a reason, he explained. It allowed the gathered mushrooms to drop their spores through the holes.

'*Ecco*! There will be many more little mushrooms.'

Davide joined in the laughter. He looked happy and relaxed, the shadows of his work and its dangers left behind. Matilde's sharp eyes had noted the ring and she asked them if they hadn't got something to tell her. Their secret was out, and on this carefree day far from the city and any possible threat, they shared their joy.

Amy helped Matilde unload a staggering amount of food, both savoury and sweet, including her own contribution of chilli con carne with spiced guacamole. They set it all out on a trestle table. Another table was crowded with bottles of wine. With Davide by her side, the others raised their glasses to fete the *fidanzati*, Amy displaying her ring for all to admire.

There was a moment when he'd gone to help Salvatore that she stood a little apart, watching everyone laughing and talking. Into her mind came the memory of last Easter, of just such an occasion when she had first met Giorgio. So much had happened in just a few months. She felt a twinge of guilt that her happiness had sacrificed his.

'Amy?' Davide was back at her side. 'Anything the matter?'

'No.'

'You seemed faraway.'

'It's nothing, really, just this season always makes me a bit nostalgic.'

She saw he was eyeing her quizzically.

'I think I've always felt like that,' she explained, 'Even as a child, though I only thought about it fairly recently.'

Into her mind came the echo of her mother's words spoken one thundery afternoon in England as they sat in the backroom of *Zest*, having a cup of tea. She had mentioned a book she'd read at Amy's age, one that had made a lasting impression on her.

'It was called *The Garden of the Finzi-Continis*, and it's the story of a first love, but only partly: there is so much more. Thinking about the difference between you and me, something in that book came back to me. Micol – she's the love interest – explains that for her the past counts far more than the present, memories are more valuable than anything tangible. She wishes that the present should immediately turn into the past, so that it could be loved and dreamed about at leisure.'

A loud rumble of thunder had made them both jump. But it was cosy in the little room, listening to the lash of rain against the windowpane obscuring the outside world, a time for confidences.

Her mother continued. 'There's our difference, I have always lived in the present and usually not brooded over it but that's never been the same with you. I remember a children's party when no one could find you. You'd turned your back on the others and were sitting on the garden swing, deep in thought, daydreaming about heaven knows what.'

Amy remembered thinking that maybe it was true. With Davide's long absence, he had become for her unreal and mythical, frighteningly unbelievable. But she had continued to dwell on their brief times together, turning them into a romantic story, so that if nothing ensued, she possessed the memory of happy times.

Had she begun to protect herself from the risk of losing Davide once again, by virtue of the dangers he ran? Was she already storing this happy September day in her bank of memories, to be retrieved should the unthinkable happen? And had her mother always lived in the present? Surely she must have retained some recollections of that summer with Marco? It was certain he had never forgotten it. Or had she deliberately blocked them out?

She was aware of Davide's voice, his arms around her, pulling her to him.

'I know,' he said softly. 'Every day must be treasured.' He stroked back her hair and kissed her. 'And I'll do my very best to make sure we have many, many more.'

'Oh Davide, Davide.'

Davide: he was engraved on her heart. Whatever happened in the future, she would never forget his name.

Amy felt his presence, solid and real. The Roman sun was warm on her neck and soon they would join her friends to feast and drink. She saw love and resolution in Davide's eyes and thrust away any thoughts of losing him. This season would not be a melancholic one but a second spring of growth and renewal with Davide.

XLVIII

The following day Davide reluctantly returned to duty. In his absence Amy found herself glancing constantly at the ring, comforting and assuring her of his return. She couldn't bear to take it off and was wearing it when she arrived at the cat sanctuary. She set about the routine of cleaning out litter trays and laying down fresh newspapers, wondering if anyone would notice. It wasn't until some time later that Susan caught sight of it and Amy was surprised by her reaction. Instead of congratulating her, she gave a little scream.

'My God you're engaged! Amy!'

Amy smiled and held up her hand. Yes, isn't it beautiful?'

Susan scarcely glanced at it. 'Who's the man? Do I know him?'

'Not really.'

The American continued to stare at her as the truth dawned. 'It's not... not that guy from Naples? Oh Amy, are you sure you know what you're doing?'

Amy was beginning to feel annoyed. 'As a matter of fact, I do.'

'From what you told me he sounded very unreliable.' Susan persisted. 'Going off without a word and you never knowing when he was coming back. I remember you being very upset about it all. A mystery man I think you called him once.'

'Its OK, it's all been clarified now.'

'Well I darn well hope so. Remember what I told you about that guy I fell for? Told me he loved me and wanted to marry me and I believed him until I found out it was all a pack of lies.'

Amy's tone sharpened. 'Davide's not like that.'

'You're sure?'

It was obvious Susan had continued to mull over the subject of Amy's engagement. Later on in the afternoon as they were preparing the feeding bowls, she broached it again.

'You do realise what you 're taking on in marrying an Italian, Amy? I've heard it from foreign women so many times. These Italian men are all sweetness and light in the early days, but that soon wears off. Then they start having a wandering eye. And remember, this is the land of Mammismo, an Italian mother will only relinquish her son into the hands of a woman whom they are sure will carry on the care and smothering love she has lavished on him. And even then she will retain the power she's always had. I'm warning you, think very carefully.'

Much later, seated by the window of the apartment, Amy pondered Susan's words. How close was Davide's attachment to his mother, she wondered. He hadn't spoken much about her except to praise her cooking and compare it favourably with that in the restaurants where they had eaten. How much would the woman become involved in their lives? She remembered Chrissie speaking of her husband Peppe. 'When you marry an Italian you marry the family,' she had said. And, of course, there was her mother's cynicism where Italian families were concerned.

She longed for Davide, to be able to ask him all these questions and to be reassured. She couldn't discuss it with Paolo for he was away once again in Menton. She imagined him in the apartment with the delightful Francois and wished them well. She waited impatiently for his return to Rome. She had planned to ask him to be a witness at their wedding and there were other preparations to be made: what she would wear, food and drink to order for a modest reception, her mother and father's arrangements for coming to Rome. They swarmed in her head but were now mixed with this fresh anxiety about the doubts Susan had sown.

******

'I got your message. Sorry I didn't call last night but I was tired after my journey. Shall we have a drink, this evening?'

'You can't make it earlier?' Amy twisted her ring. 'This morning, say? I could give the spice stall a miss, if you could.'

'Oh dear, it sounds urgent. Shall we say Tazza d'Oro? Eleven?'

Amy hurried past Largo Argentina on her way to the now-familiar coffee house near Piazza Navona. As always, the smell of dark roasted coffee hit her as soon as she walked through the doors of Tazza D'Oro. She glanced at the busy roasting machines, the shelves stacked with bags of coffee, before spotting Paolo who was standing at the counter.

'*Granita di caffe?*' he asked with a smile.

He knew how she loved the dreamy mix of frozen coffee, broken into slush and layered with fresh whipped cream, the bitterness cut by the dairy sweetness, it's heavenly taste.

Seated, he took out his pack of brown cigarettes and lit one. His gaze went to her ring. 'Ah, so something very important has happened.'

'Yes, I'm engaged to be married, Paolo, to Davide.'

'My congratulations.'

Amy sniffed and fumbled in her bag for a tissue.

'Come now, Amy, surely this is something to be happy about.' Over the rim of his coffee cup, he eyed her keenly. 'Or are there complications?'

As always, his prescience struck her. He had this way of guessing her thoughts and feelings that she found extraordinary.

'People, well one person, has queried that I am going into this without realising I shall be taking on a bossy mother in law as well as Davide.'

Paolo merely grunted.

'I've been worrying about it, of how your mother interfered and ruined my mother and Marco's relationship. She disliked Mum because she was a foreigner and made it her business to get rid of her.'

There was a pause. Paolo was obviously thinking.

'I understand,' he said at last. 'Some Italian mothers find it impossible to truly let their sons go. Mine was one of them. She always wanted to rule Marco's life, not mine, of course, but all the same she made things very unpleasant for me. But not every-one is like that, Amy cara. From the little you have told me of Davide, I guess he flew the nest some time ago.' He smiled. 'I'm sure he won't criticise your pasta sauce or the way his shirts are ironed. He probably does his own laundry, anyway. I have always been like that since I escaped to live my life the way I chose, always very independent.'

Amy said 'I hope you're right.' The weight seemed to have lifted a little. 'And I do love him.'

Paolo took out another cigarette. 'Well then?'

The taste of the granita had conjured memories of other occasions when she had met Paolo at Tazza d'Oro. The first time it had been when she was newly arrived in Rome, expecting it to be only a brief visit. Paolo had persuaded her to give Rome a few more days. She had thought of the shadowy room in the apartment, of the previous evening, when she had sat watching the nightlife of the city from the big window that looked down onto the square. She'd remembered her mother's reaction and been incredulous that anyone could turn down such a wonderful gift. During this initial brief meeting, a subtle shift seemed to have occurred. The feeling of having only a fleeting purpose in this city had been replaced by a sense of connection.

Months later she had decided to leave, to summon the courage to move on, as her mother had done. Yet she was still torn, still clinging to vain shreds of hope, the stubborn belief in happy endings. Once again, it was Paolo who had been there for her. This time, he hadn't tried to dissuade her but he promised that the apartment would remain hers to visit whenever she came back to Rome. The reopening of a stall would not be a problem, his contact would see to that. Now on this third occasion, he was supporting her once again. Amy was filled with love for this man who had been like a father to her. She knew he had suffered early persecution for being gay. He had loved, lost and loved again but, unlike his brother, he had never let it destroy him. 'Our life will never be perfect, but it will be full of wonders.' he had told her once. Now he was sharing her happiness with no sense of bitterness.

'Thank you, Paolo,' she said. '*Mille grazie.*'

'Don't mention it,' he shrugged. 'Another granita?'

She made a face.

'Ah, you can manage one. This is a special occasion.'

When he returned to the table, she asked him if he would be a witness at their wedding ceremony in Bracciano.

'I should be delighted and honoured. Thank you. By the way, where are you two going to live?'

Amy took a breath. 'We were wondering if you would allow us to stay on in the apartment. Of course, I'd understand if you preferred us not to, but Davide loves it as much as I do.'

She saw there were tears in Paolo's eyes. He fetched out his usual snowy handkerchief to wipe them away. 'But of course, you must. Where else? I am sure Marco if he were still alive would be so happy that love has returned to that place after all its sadness.'

XLIX

Usually, Giulia loved her monthly appointment with Andrea, her hairdresser. She basked in these hours of being pampered, of being brought magazines and coffee by Magda, his assistant, in the warm, scented atmosphere of the salon. But today's 'roots, trim and conditioner' was an impromptu event, driven by Amy's invitation to meet her mother. Caroline would be arriving in Rome for the wedding and they'd agreed that a preliminary rendezvous might make it easier to come face to face on the actual day. For once Giulia found it difficult to relax or to pay proper attention to Andrea's chat. Her stomach churned with the anticipation of this meeting. She had a memory of her once rival as a leggy young beauty with long, blonde hair on the one occasion she had glimpsed her with Marco. It was difficult to imagine her as a middle-aged woman. And what would Caroline think of her? Giulia was not vain but she took care of her appearance, unlike some of her friends who were now middle-aged matrons with grandchildren. She supposed they might be forgiven for relaxing standards and making less effort.

Andrea was showing her the finished result in the hand mirror. There was not a trace of grey. Her friend Carla envied her for being well turned out. All the same she found meeting the Englishwoman a daunting prospect.

At home once more she prepared a simple lunch, finding it hard to concentrate on anything more elaborate. She watched Gian Franco eat with appetite, regardless it seemed of the impending encounter.

'Not hungry?' was his only comment.

Giulia laid down her fork. 'I'm nervous,' she said. 'I don't know what to expect.'

'Of this Caroline woman, why should you be? If anything, it is she who should be feeling nervous, coming back to Rome, after all these years. Meeting her future son in law for the first time, that's enough to make anyone nervous.'

Giulia took a gulp of wine. 'I know all that but…'

'Anyway, Amy has chosen you as a witness, that counts for something.'

'Yes, Gian Franco, but she was very attractive, a real *bambola*.'

Her husband grunted. 'My dear Giulia, that was, what over thirty years ago. I bet she's fat and wrinkly now.' There was unusual spite in his voice.

Giulia switched subject. 'I don't know what to wear.'

Gian Franco sighed. You women!' He cast a longing glance at the silent television screen. In the next half an hour a quiz show would start, possibly hosted by the delicious Selina. 'Go!' he said. 'Change into whatever and go and get it over with. I'll take care of the washing up.'

Surprised, Giulia rose from the table and did as she was told.

******

At first sight, Giulia glimpsed traces of the girl Caroline had once been. Her hair was still long although its blondness was obviously no longer natural. She was certainly not fat but there were deep creases running down from her nose to mouth, crows feet wrinkles around her eyes and puckered lines on her upper lip. All signs, Giulia thought, of a heavy smoker.

Amy has arranged to meet them at the Protestant Cemetery. 'Mum's never been there so I thought it would be a nice, quiet place for us to get together.'

Giulia felt her heart race as she neared the couple standing just inside the entrance and wondered if this meeting was such a good idea. She need not have worried. The years appeared to have mellowed Caroline and it was she who made the first friendly gesture as Amy introduced them.

'Giulia, I may call you Giulia? I've heard so much about you from Amy. How are you? I'm afraid my Italian is a little rusty,' she laughed. 'I haven't used it in a long time.'

'Please don't apologise. If only my English was as good.'

They discussed Caroline's journey to Rome and where she would be staying during her trip.

'Amy took me to this lovely restaurant last night and I ate the best Amatriciana I've had in years.'

Food steered Giulia onto safer ground. Here she knew what she was talking about.

'Where was that?' she turned to Amy.

'Grappolo d'Oro.'

'Ah yes, I know of it. I think they always use the very best guanciale.'

'And chillies, eh darling?' she appealed to her daughter who was looking openly relieved the meeting seemed to be going well. 'Amy's the expert on spices, you see, Giulia. She's far superior to me.'

Into Giulia's mind crept the image of the two of them, she and Gian Franco, sprawled on the sofa, mouths afire after her mistaken use of Amy's curry mixture. She had been mortified when Amy had explained the packet contained enough spices for six curries not one.

'She's taught me a great deal,' she said. 'You have a wonderful daughter, Caroline. She has been a blessing to me. I envy you.'

'I know, I'm lucky to have her.'

Embarrassed, Amy suggested they move on into the cemetery where she pointed out several of the more interesting graves. Caroline was struck by the weeping angel statue, which she remembered seeing in a book. They paused by the twin graves of Keats and his friend Severn and then Amy, with a swift glance at Giulia as if for approval, guided them to the site of Marco's grave.

'This is where he's buried,' she said.

Caroline, who had been chatting away and happily absorbing her surroundings, fell silent. She stood for a long time gazing at the epitaph that Giulia knew so well.

At last Caroline spoke: 'That is so sad, so very sad.'

'Yes,' said Giulia, 'It surely is.'

'You loved him too, didn't you Giulia?'

'We both did.'

Caroline raised her head to meet Giulia's gaze. 'Ah but it was I who destroyed him, not you.'

For a moment there was silence as the two women turned their full attention to the grave, sharing the memory of the young vibrant man riding his Vespa through the streets of Rome, impetuous, life loving Marco. To think they were both at his grave.

'It wasn't your fault, Caroline. It was the fault of his mother. It was *Signora* Giordano who destroyed his happiness.'

'Oh Giulia!'

The two women embraced while a startled Amy looked on.

It was Giulia who took command of the situation. 'Come now, enough of this sadness. We must be happy for Amy and Davide and their new life together. Let's go to the café across the road for a beautiful espresso.'

She and Amy led the way among the box hedges and rows of tombs and Caroline, who had hesitated for a last look, followed them.

'Look!' she exclaimed, pointed up to the sky where forked tailed swallows darted restlessly, preparing to migrate. 'Swallows! I've never forgotten the swallows.'

L

Amy would always remember those few days spent with her mother when they discovered a new and more intimate bond between them. Caroline had arrived in Rome a week before her husband. Bernard would join them two days before the wedding and Davide would be unable to return to Rome until a day later. Thus the two women spent time together ostensibly making preparations for the Big Day but also wandering round the city as Caroline reacquainted herself with the scenes of her youth. They spent one morning together at Amy's spice stall when she introduced her mother to Salvatore and Matilde. Caroline joined with them in admiration of the stall's success, her Italian coming back by leaps and bounds. At Caroline's suggestion they took the train to Frascati one evening where she guided Amy to the bright lights of the *norcineria* in the ancient centre to buy thick slices of seasoned pork. Amy inhaled the rich spicy smell, watching as the butcher carved the meat. Next a stop at the bakery for crusty bread before her mother led her to an *osteria*. They settled outside at a battered table and ordered a carafe of chilled white wine.

'Marco brought me here when I first met him. I remember asking him if they minded us bringing our own food?' Caroline said. 'His friend, the owner of the cellar told me it is a very old custom going back to at least medieval times. Winemakers hung out a laurel branch when the new wine was ready. People would flock to drink and celebrate the wine. They brought their snacks to soak it up and as these were usually salty and spicy, that led to ordering yet another jug, so everyone was satisfied.' She laughed but Amy saw the expression in her eyes.

'It's not too painful for you, Mum, coming back here?'

Her mother shook her head. 'This has made me remember the happy days I spent with Marco, such happy days. Up until now I've focussed on what came later.'

Amy raised her glass. 'Let's drink to the happy days.'

By tacit agreement neither of them spoke of a visit to Monte Verde but they walked in the Borghese gardens, which had been pivotal in both their lives. They sat by the lake whose surface sparkled with points of light and gave back to the weeping willows an upside-down facsimile of themselves.

'I came to sit here on the feast of Maria Goretti,' Caroline said. 'It was Signora Giordano's name day and they were having a family lunch to which I wasn't invited. Marco didn't particularly want to go either but he made a self-righteous remark that should have rung warning bells.'

'Oh?'

'He said that here in Italy the family is the family and he had to respect his elders, meaning, of course, his mother.' She laughed wryly. 'I thought then I'd better not meet them. Anyway, I came to sit here but my mind was elsewhere. I imagined Marco and his family settling down to a large lunch. He'd already told me what a fantastic cook his mother was. I kept wondering whether Lia was there, smiling and unaware of what lay in store. When would he tell them he was in love with someone else? Would he speak of me? That was the time when I was studying, or trying to study that book I told you about, *The Garden of the Finzi-Continis*. I'd brought it here in the hope my mind would be distracted. But all I could think of how Marco's would take it.'

For a moment they were silent, dwelling on the image of the young Caroline who was convinced her future was about to change.

Amy spoke at last: 'If you could have known then how Signora Giordano would've reacted, would you have acted differently?'

Caroline smiled and reached for her cigarettes. She blew a ring of smoke into the still air. 'Darling, I was young and in love. All I could think about was Marco and when I would see him again. The day I came here, was the day I realised I loved him and that I'd changed from the girl who was fancy free and always on the move to something new. It was a frightening feeling.'

It was Amy's turn to reminisce. 'I came here with Paolo, about this time last year. You'd been on the phone asking me how much longer I was going to stay in Rome and I didn't know what to do. Davide had left Rome and I wondered if I would ever see him again.' She recalled how Paolo had weighed up the situation. He'd wondered if life here in Rome was not turning out the way I'd hoped. 'Maybe I needed more of a challenge.'

Caroline inhaled deeply 'Good old Paolo, it was what I was saying at the time,'

'He asked me how old I was and said that many women my age thought about marrying and having children.' Amy laughed. 'He sounded so much like you, Mum! I told him I'd had such a protected life that I wanted to have a go at travelling. You did, you went all over the place so why shouldn't I?'

She met her mother's gaze. 'But you didn't, did you, Amy? Travel, I mean. You just came here and stayed.'

'I know. Oh I used to hear friends talking about all the places they'd been. I listened to your travel tales but when it came to the point of actually taking off, I somehow didn't have the courage.'

'And what was the wise Paolo's response to that?'

Amy paused, recalling Paolo's remark. 'It is not always a question of courage but being true to yourself. You may have a passing resemblance to your mother, but your character is very different.'

Amy watched some children feeding the ducks while their smiling parents looked on. She felt a stab of sadness that she would never see a son of her own doing the same. She would not repeat Paolo's summing up of her mother's character, that she was incapable of patience and adaptability.

'He said that life is a journey and no one knows where it takes us. He told me that he had loved, lost and loved again but, unlike Marco, he had never let it destroy hm. I should follow my heart, he said, even at the risk of its being broken.'

'But it hasn't been, has it?' Her mother's tone was curt as if she wanted to brush off the subject of broken hearts. 'You're marrying this Davide, who I've yet to meet. I just hope I'll like him.'

'Oh, you will, Mum, you will. He's... he's wonderful.'

Caroline smiled. 'You might be a little biased, darling,' She rose from the bench. 'All this talking's made me thirsty, shall we go to the little café if its still there, and get a drink?'

Following her, Amy began to feel uneasy. Suppose her mother and Davide didn't get on? She'd never bargained for that.

The following day they got down to the business of buying Amy's dress. She had no idea of what style to choose and was relieved when her mother took command.

'I've done a bit of research and I think I know just the shop. It's not far from Piazza Navona in via del Governo Vecchio.'

'Mum, surely that's a very expensive area!'

'Not at all, the prices seemed very reasonable and anyway, it's not your concern. I'm buying it for you.'

As Amy began to protest, her mother continued: 'Take it as a wedding present from Zest, we've done very well this year.'

Feeling rather as if she had returned to her childhood Amy meekly followed her mother who led the way to the little cobbled street lined with boutique shops. She halted before one of them. Amy thought it looked very exclusive.

'Come on, Amy! My daughter's a little nervous,' she explained to the elegant older woman who ushered them in.

'It's natural, signorina, on such an occasion.' The woman was surveying her with practised eyes and Amy felt herself blush. 'Such a pretty figure the young lady has,' she concluded. 'Let us find her something that will show it off to the best advantage.'

She disappeared into a back room while Amy gave her mother an agonised look. 'I want to escape,' it said.

'Don't be silly, Amy, this will be fun.'

'And expensive.'

'Stop thinking about money! You're like your father, always putting a price on everything. This is a one off and I don't care how much I spend.'

The reappearance of the woman with a sheath of dresses over her arm interrupted them. ''If the young lady would like to try these?'

'Well, go on, Amy!' her mother muttered when Amy still hesitated.

As she stepped out of her blouse and skirt and before the woman slipped the first of the dresses over her head Amy wished she'd worn the luxurious underwear she'd bought when Davide had spent his final week with her last year. The woman however appeared not to notice her everyday bra and knickers, fastening the buttons, fussing over the set of the shoulders and straightening the skirt before turning her round to look in the mirror. At once she saw the dress, though beautifully made, was too elaborate with its big puffed sleeves and ruched bodice.

'You don't like?' The woman met her reflected expression

'Not really.'

'OK try this one.'

The second was too severe with its high neckline and slim fit but the third... simple and elegant, in white lace with a boat neckline and long sleeves, it looked as if it had been made for her. Amy stared in amazement at the glamorous stranger in the glass.

'Beautiful,' came the woman's voice behind her. 'Just beautiful, and see how the low V of the back shows off your pretty shoulders. Allora, this is the dress for you, without a doubt.'

As she emerged, her mother gave a gasp of admiration. 'Darling, you look like a princess.'

Amy smiled. 'Well I am marrying my prince.' She saw there were tears in her mother's eyes.

LI

Two days later they stood in Fiumicino airport waiting for her father to arrive. The flight was late and Caroline became impatient.

'He'll be here soon,' Amy soothed.

'That is if he's even managed to get himself onto the plane. You know your Dad, he's hardly a world traveller, in fact he's scarcely been out of England.'

Amy began to feel slightly annoyed with her mother. She always enjoyed a trip to an airport, the sense of being caught up in all the comings and goings, the line of destinations flashing up on the boards. She loved to people watch, noting the varying way folk dressed when travelling, some immaculately turned out, others scruffy, new arrivals still wearing flip flops and sunhats as if unwilling to relinquish their holiday identity. She recalled again Paolo's definition of her mother's character as lacking patience and adaptability.

'Ah here he is at last!' Caroline's voice interrupted these thoughts.

Amy caught sight of a man who wore a military style short-sleeve jacket that was long and belted, over a matching pair of wide trousers and for a moment didn't recognise it was her father.

'Oh my God!' her mother murmured 'He's dug out his old safari suit and…' she gave an exasperated sigh. 'Just take a look at his feet he's wearing white socks and his bowling shoes! Whatever possessed him?'

Among the jeans and tee shirt crowd coming off the plane he certainly looked a fashion oddity.

Ignoring this Amy waved and called 'Dad! Dad! Over here.'

The bewildered expression on his face cleared and he came towards them, wheeling a dilapidated brown suitcase.

'Thank heavens you're here,' he said. 'I don't know what I'd have done if you weren't.'

Caroline clicked her tongue. 'Bernard, of course we'd be here. What do you take us for?'

'I was worried, the plane was late and I thought you might not wait.'

'Never mind, you're here now Dad and it's lovely to see you.'

'And you, Amy. My goodness you've…'

It almost seemed he was going to say 'grown' but he continued: 'changed, you're quite the smart young lady.'

They smiled at one another and Amy felt a camaraderie she had rarely experienced before.

'We've missed you, you know?' he said.

'And I've missed you. I'm so glad you could make it.'

'Can't miss my only daughter's wedding, now can I?'

'Bernard!' Caroline interrupted. 'Where on earth did you find that suit? I thought you'd got rid of it, years ago.'

To Amy's surprise, her father gave her a conspiratorial wink. 'Ah my dear you don't know everything about me, even if you think you do.'

'Obviously not it seems. Come on let's get a move on. I don't want us to miss the train.' She led the way to the nearest lift.

Amy felt her father catch her sleeve. He spoke in a low voice. 'I hope I'm not expected to eat a lot of strange food, Amy, you know, this continental breakfast malarkey' He sounded worried.

She was reminded of her mother's attempts to make him enjoy the spicy Eastern dishes she'd learned on a cookery course. Bernard Armstrong preferred the dishes of his schooldays: shepherd's pie, sausage and chips and jam roly-poly pudding.

'I'm sure the hotel can come up with a full English,' she said. 'I'll make sure they do.'

'Thank you.' He looked relieved.

'Come along you two!' Caroline, several paces ahead, was waving train tickets. 'Do you intend to hang around here all day? There's a lot to do.'

It was later than she planned before Amy put the key in her door and let herself into the silent apartment. Having settled her parents into the Hotel Sans Souci and confirmed that, indeed, the signor could have as comprehensive an English breakfast as he desired, she'd prepared to leave.

But her father insisted she eat dinner with them. 'I've had a squint at the menu here and it seems a pretty decent choice, I don't see the point of going out to a restaurant.'

In the charming dining room where each table was set with pink cloths and vases of roses he ordered sparkling wine.

'My daughter's getting married the day after tomorrow,' he told the waiter, who shook his hand and congratulated him, as if it had been all his doing.

In the time-honoured manner of the Englishman abroad, Bernard had adopted a loud voice, enunciating every syllable.

'I'm sure he understands English perfectly,' Caroline muttered. 'Don't make a fool of yourself, Bernard.'

But he was in celebratory mode and would not be deflated.

'How are things at the shop?' her mother wanted to know. 'Is that girl Alison running things properly?'

Her husband was gazing round the room and appeared not to be listening. 'Know something?' he remarked. 'I'm quite taking to this foreign lark. They all seem such a friendly bunch.'

'That depends,' said her mother.

Amy noted the old subterranean antagonism between her parents, something she had learned to live with from childhood, a subtle clash of personalities. The only difference now it seemed, was that her father was holding his own. The new solidarity she had felt with him, that afternoon, intensified. He was curious to hear about her life in Rome, her work at the cat sanctuary.

'It must be quite something to live surrounded by so much antiquity, or do you get used to it? I think I will take a stroll round the principal monuments tomorrow,' he continued. 'The Forum, the Colosseum and so on. You don't mind, do you, Caroline? I know you'll be busy helping Amy and I'd only get in the way.'

Caroline was reaching in her bag for her cigarettes. The waiter leapt forward with a lighter. She waved him away and produced her own, a gold Ronson.

'You can go where ever you like, Bernard,' she said. 'As long as you promise not to wear that awful suit, again.'

LII

Amy counted the chimes of the Santa Maria Maggiore bells: one, two, three… eleven. She was still wide-awake, seated by the apartment window, gazing out into the night. She remembered Davide telling her about one of the church's bells, a special one called La Sperduta. It tolled every night at nine and was the stuff of a local legend, dating back to the 16th century. 'A girl was lost in the area and turned to the Virgin Mary for help. In reply the bell started to ring and she was able to follow the sound to safety.'

On an August evening, last year, Amy had sat here in despair, hearing the chimes of La Sperduta. Davide had left, the day before, giving her no idea whether he would or could return. She had felt lost and very alone then. But now… I should be feeling happy, she scolded herself. I should be going to bed. Instead she remained by the window gazing down on the emptying square, hearing the church bells toll the passing hours. She was in nostalgic mood. This would be the very last evening she would spend alone in this place that had become her haven. Tomorrow Davide would be arriving and her mother was bound to fuss, urging her to double check all the details of her wedding day. Tomorrow evening there would be no sitting up until midnight if she were to look her best the next day. Amy glanced behind her at the shadowy room lit only by the lamp on the low table. Her gaze fell on the telephone, which Paolo had so thoughtfully installed for her, anxious she might feel vulnerable alone. How many times had it shrilled from England with her mother, saying that her stay in Rome was a pleasant interlude and it was time she came home? On other occasions she had longed for it to ring and to hear Davide's voice again but it had remained obstinately silent. Her time in Rome had been a seesaw of confidence in her new life and the success she had made of the spice stall and doubt as to whether it was all an illusion, an ephemeral bubble that would eventually burst. The sofa with its plumped up cushions looked inviting. She thought of those evenings when she had sat there to watch *Un Posto al Sole*. She had become addicted to this soap opera, marvelling at the beautiful locations, the splendid bay of Naples, and she had become immersed in the story of love and betrayal at the exquisite villa.

Next morning, any idea of leaving had faded as she watched another day dawn over the city, renewing her love of Rome and the man she had met here, knowing she must stay on in the hope her future would be revealed.

This room when she had first arrived in Rome had seemed to reverberate the melancholy of a man who could never forget his lost love. She had imagined evenings when Marco must have done what she was doing now, gazing from this window as another day died and memories of the short time he had spent with her mother had overwhelmed him. But as the months passed this sensation had faded to be replaced by the welcoming feeling of coming home when the day was done.

She remembered the first night she had invited Davide to the apartment and how, at the last minute she had turned away from their lovemaking. Into her mind had come the image of her mother and Marco. But the next time Davide came back into her life, they had united in a frenzied surrender to desire. A night followed of passion and delight that they would never forget, and that finally beached them into an exhausted and satiated sleep. 'Ah Davide,' she murmured and longed to feel his arms around her, holding her close.

The church bells struck midnight and Amy stirred herself from her reverie. Her wedding dress hung ghostlike on the back of the door, confirming the reality of her future with Davide whatever it might hold for them. Tomorrow she would hear his voice and see the love in his eyes. She was about to go to bed when the phone rang. To her surprise, it was Paolo.

'I know it's late but I had this feeling you might still be awake,' he said, as always with his uncanny way of reading her state of mind. 'I just wanted to tell you not to worry, I know all will be well. I've told you before, you have the right qualities, dear Amy, of patience and adaptability, you will succeed in this marriage where your mother's relationship with Marco failed.'

The benevolence in his words was so affecting, Amy had to swallow before she spoke. 'Thank you, Paolo, you are a dear.'

'And remember, not only I, all your friends will always be with you, cara. We love you.'

When Amy finally settled down to sleep, the bells of Santa Maria Maggiore struck one.

LIII

'I haven't listened to you, this time,' Giulia told Gian
Franco.

He had just returned from the market, jubilant because
he had secured some beautiful fresh figs at a bargain
price as the stallholder was preparing to finish for the
day. He had expected a grateful welcome, not the
determined expression on his wife's face. Tenderly he
laid the delicate fruit on the table and stood back to
admire them.

'An old dress might have done for that christening,'
Giulia continued. 'But I've ordered a new outfit for
Amy's wedding and that's that. I shall pick it up this
afternoon.'

As this appeared to be a *fatto compiuto*, Gian Franco
merely shrugged. He couldn't wait to bite into a fig and
taste the golden juice that stored all the sweetness of
summer.

'Well aren't you going to ask me what it's like?'

'Does it matter what I think? You obviously like it.'

Giulia sighed and glanced at the clock. She turned off
the oven. 'If I walked around with a cardboard box over
my head I don't think you'd notice.'

This image of Giulia was so ludicrous that Gian
Franco sniggered and even his wife suppressed a smile.

'You know what I mean,' she said at last. 'You never voice any opinion.'

'Tesoro, you should know by now I'm not really a judge of women's fashion. You always look nice to me.'

'Nice' she spat the word as if it were an insult. 'I want to look more than nice. I want to look... splendid.'

'And you will, I'm sure.' He eyed the pasta sauce, which must now be cooling. Gently he added: 'but remembered this is Amy's day. You don't want to outshine the bride.'

'Much chance of that, Amy is a lovely girl.'

Gian Franco came up behind her and slid his arms round her waist. 'And you are my lovely girl. Now let's eat and you can tell me about this outfit of yours.'

When she had stood in the changing room of Le Sorelle Isabella last week trying on one outfit after another, debating which colour suited her or whether she was too old to get away with a certain style, she was reminded of a day many years ago.

******

Somehow her mother has discovered that Caroline had finished with Marco and left Rome. When Giulia had questioned this, her mother told her that she'd had a call from *Signora* Giordano, who, it seemed, had felt it her duty to tell her. The two women had discussed the situation at length.

283

'You see, I told you if you hung around, things would come right. Oh, he'll pine for a bit but he'll come to see sense.'

'But what about Gian Franco?' Giulia interrupted this triumphant chatter. The friendship between them was becoming more intimate and she had begun to feel that her future might not be so bleak.

'Oh him!' Her mother made a gesture of pushing the invisible Gian Franco away. 'You can get rid of him.'

'That would be so cruel. He's been so kind and understanding.'

'You must forget all these scruples, girl! If you want to get anywhere in this world you'll have to toughen up.'

Giulia had never realised until now quite how ruthless her mother could be. Was it because her own marriage had been a disappointment and that she was investing her aspirations on her daughter?

'Now don't rush things,' her mother was advising. 'Marco will get over this girl, eventually, he has to, just bide your time. Meanwhile, we'll work on your style a little, smooth the rough edges.'

In spite of her guilt over Gian Franco and her misgivings that Marco had ceased to be interested in her, indeed had never seen her as a prospective wife, the tiny flame of hope was fanned again. Suppose her mother was right, suppose Marco realised it was better to have an Italian wife who would fit in with his family? It might, it could happen, couldn't it? She began to imagine how it would be if he began to ask her out again. She would become more daring, take his arm as she had seen other girls do, smile with her eyes, even flirt a little. She would set out to charm Marco. She allowed herself to dream of her wedding. It would be a glamorous affair with the wealth of the Giordano family behind it. There would be photographs in the society pages of magazines, an expensive honeymoon before they settled down to married life and children.

Her mother appeared to have similar dreams. Giulia would need to lose a few kilos if she were to fit into the designer clothes she would be wearing. She served her daughter smaller portions of pasta and made up with large salads and fruit. She took her to a beauty salon for manicures, preparing her hands for the eventual engagement ring. She even allowed her into her kitchen to be taught the principles of Roman cuisine.

Caught up in this fantasy, Giulia went to Le Sorelle Isabella and stared at wedding dresses displayed in its windows. One day she plucked up courage and went inside to try some of them on. There was one that caught her fancy and she stayed in the changing room for a long time, admiring herself in the mirror, until an assistant tapped politely on the door. She asked if the *signorina* needed any help.

Together they admired the dress, the deep v neckline that gave a hint of Giulia's full breasts, the fluted style, which, while accentuating her trim waist and hips, floated about her legs and feet in creamy waves. It was all she could do to take it off, tell the assistant she would consider it and step out into the everyday streets.

******

Giulia came to herself, meeting the reflection of a middle-aged woman in the glass with a wry smile. What a hopeless romantic she had been, clinging on to a cause lost long ago. And romantics, as she had told Amy, often suffered. Life for the young Englishwoman would not be easy. She was turning her back on her native culture to embrace another that was still in some ways unknown to her. But she was following her dream and marrying for love and Giulia wished her well with all her heart.

It was time to come to a decision. She opted for a dress and jacket in a duck egg shade, which showed off, but did not overly expose, her still trim body. The assistant noted a few small alterations to be made and complimented her on her choice, saying how well it suited her olive skin colouring.

LIV

In the afternoon before her wedding Amy slipped away on a private mission. She had spent a busy morning, first with Giulia and Matilde who had undertaken to oversee the food for the reception. Later over a snack lunch she and her mother went through the list they had made, to make sure nothing had been forgotten.

'I think Rome's gone to Bernard's head,' Caroline remarked. 'He was off out early to see the sights and then planned to sit in a café with a bottle of wine. It's quite extraordinary.'

Amy remembered that sense of connection she had felt with her father, the night before. She recalled a remark he'd made over a year ago. It was on the night before she left England for her new life in Rome. Dad had taken them out to a carvery for a farewell dinner. To her surprise he'd told her he envied her courage. His destiny had been mapped out from an early age. "I thought that life might be more than bread and circuses", he had said. Maybe, like her, he had been bewitched by the allure of the city on this brief trip to Rome, Amy thought. It would be he rather than her mother who made future trips to Rome.

'I suppose I should spend a little time with him, this afternoon,' her mother was saying. 'That is, as long as you don't need me, darling. I'll pop back later with the 'something borrowed' you need to wear, tomorrow. Have you got the 'something blue?' I know, I am hopelessly superstitious!' she added when Amy shook her head, smiling.

Davide would not arrive until early evening and she was looking forward to a few hours on her own, besides, there was something she needed to do. It had come to her out of the blue, the memory of that first visit to St Michael's, Father Bruno's church and the vision she had had there. Now on the brink of her marriage she felt the need to return as if to complete her story in a suitable way: a story that had begun with her first meeting with Davide, the brief time they'd had together and the loss of hope in the ensuing months when, at her lowest ebb, she had entered the church. As Amy crossed the bridge and entered the cobbled streets of Trastevere, she noticed the September sunshine was hazy. Several people were wearing jackets once more and some even wore scarves. The leaves of the trees lining via Cola di Rienzo were wearing their second palette of the seasons: russet, purple amber and red with a hint of gold. Autumn was well on its way. She found the church with ease and passed through the garden where a few roses still hung on the bushes. The door to St Michael's was shut and for a moment she feared it might be locked but it opened at her touch. Dust motes danced in the beam of light coming through the stained glass windows and lay lozenges of colour on the uneven floor. She came to stand before the gilded mosaic of the six-winged angel, its wings decorated with peacock's eyes. On that other occasion, as she gazed she had seemed to move into a timeless space and, as if from nowhere, there came an overwhelming sense of certainty, dispelling all doubts or hesitations, and she had experienced a crystal-clear vision of what was important in her life. She knew she loved Davide, and she trusted she would see him again. All would be revealed. She must be patient and wait.

Moments passed and nothing like that happened this time. Amy realised she had come this afternoon seeking more reassurance. She concentrated her whole being on the angel. Nothing.

'Oh please,' she murmured 'please.'

'Signorina, are you troubled?' She turned at the sound of a voice and saw it was the rosy-faced priest who loved cats.

Amy smiled. 'It's just I'm a little nervous. I'm getting married tomorrow and...'

'And you were hoping for some divine encouragement?' Father Bruno suggested.

'Something like that but it's nonsense really. I'm marrying the man I love.'

'And he loves you?'

'Oh yes, but I'm a foreigner marrying an Italian, you see, moving into a different way of life. It's just I was hoping for... well, for some inspiration: as I've had in this church in the past.' She indicated the angel. 'I was given hope and surety that things would work out, and that Davide ad I would be together.'

Father Bruno came closer. 'Our Lord has a law of giving and receiving. Perhaps it is now time for you to sow rather than reap. Your love for each other will radiate to those around you reflecting His love. Remember what He said: 'As you sow, so you will reap.' That love will be returned to you a hundred fold.'

He turned her back to the winged angel 'You can be sure, He has not deserted you.' He indicated the inscription: He shall cover thee with His feathers and under His wings shalt thou trust: His truth shall be thy shield and buckler.

He glanced at his watch. 'You must excuse me it is time I fed my mici.'

More time had passed than Amy had realised. Fearful now that Davide might have arrived at the apartment and found her absent, she rushed through the cooling afternoon. There was no one there. She sighed with relief, then caught sight of the note. It was in her mother's handwriting. *Davide came while I was waiting for you. We are in the café across the road.* Oh no, this was an unrehearsed meeting she did not want to happen.

In her anxiety she failed to see them, then someone waved and she saw it was her mother beckoning her over. The two of them were seated at a corner table and as she approached Davide pushed back his chair and rose to kiss her.

'How long have you been waiting?' she asked him.

The half empty bottle of wine was her answer. She glanced from one to the other and saw they were both smiling.

'Caroline's been telling me about Rome in the sixties,' Davide told her. 'The hey-day of the Via Veneto. It sounded amazing.'

'Ah but it wasn't always Dolce Vita!'

Davide winked at Amy. 'I don't believe you!'

Amy relaxed, nodding and smiling, content to stay quiet and listen to their exchange. Father Bruno had been right. The love between her and Davide had expanded to embrace her mother. There had been no need to worry. All would be well.

Not long after this, her mother stubbed out her last cigarette.

'Time I left you two in peace. My husband has ordered a special meal for us at the hotel,' she told Davide. 'It's a shame you couldn't join us but...' she looked down at their hands clasped below the table. 'I think you'd rather be alone.'

'She's nice, your mother,' Davide said as they watched her willowy figure thread its way among the tables and pause to thank the waiter before disappearing down the street. He glanced at his watch. 'Shall we go?'

In the street he turned to Amy and took her in his arms. 'I've been longing to do this.'

Amy closed her eyes and leant against his firm body, smelled his familiar scent. 'Oh Davide, my love.'

He sensed her hunger and continued to hold her against him, oblivious of the evening crowds. 'I know,' he murmured. 'I'd like to come back to the apartment and spend the night with you. But tomorrow is our wedding day so it is not possible.'

Amy murmured: 'Why?'

'Something else you don't know about Italy,' he said. 'It's an old tradition that the groom stays away from his bride the night before. My mother reminded me of this.'

'Your mother?' Would she be at the wedding, she wondered.

Davide shook his head.

'But surely…'

'No my darling, she won't be there.'

Was this to be another hurdle? Did his mother disapprove of the match? Too late now to worry but maybe something she'd have to face in future.

'I'll explain some time but not now.' He laughed. 'We both need to get a good night's sleep. I can assure you there'll be no old fashioned serenade beneath your window.'

LV

The following day passed in a blur of impressions. Grey morning light, autumnal mist shrouding the spires of Santa Maria Maggiore. Strong coffee and the sweetness of a custard cream filled cornetto her mother persuaded her to eat. Her reflected face in the old mirror pale and wide eyed, the face of a stranger, one about to embark on something dangerous. Her mother's soothing voice as she settled the dress, arranging Amy's hair to take the simple ringlet of flowers.

Outside a warming of the atmosphere, sun filtering through the mist, rosy on the old buildings, orange across a slated roof, glimpses of the Tiber like polished silver. A road among trees, a shaft of light through leaves, dapple of sun and shadow on the road ahead.

A small group of people was waiting in the square of Bracciano as if for a signal to file into the wedding hall. Friendly faces: Salvatore, Matilde, Giulia and Gian Franco. And there was her father talking to Paolo elegant in a grey morning suit. It was dim inside the ancient building but then she saw him. And all the disjointed sensations of the day came together blending to create a single focus: Davide. He put his hand over hers and she gazed at him, seeing the eyes, the mouth she knew so well.

'Ready?' He murmured.

She felt as she might feel, standing at the edge of a high cliff, looking down onto a sea running between rocks, a mixture of awe and exhilaration. She took a deep breath and nodded. 'Oh yes.'

The sun was setting over the lake, flaming it with reflected light, when Paolo found her. Amy had slipped away from the celebrations to gaze at its tranquil beauty.

'Well done cara,' he murmured. She didn't understand. With a wave of his hand he indicated the restaurant garden hung with lanterns and noisy with happy laughter. 'You've brought us all together, don't you see, all the characters in your story. You've given us a happy ending, I'm sure Marco would have been proud of you.'

I suppose I have, she thought. Mum has made peace with Giulia and she's crazy about Davide. Dad has discovered an affinity with Rome and I, she glanced at her ring, I've married the man I never stopped loving. 'But it was you who persuaded me to give Rome a chance.' she insisted.

For a moment they were quiet remembering that first meeting when, had she known it, her future hung in balance. It seemed a world of experiences had happened since.

She reached up to kiss him on the cheek. 'Thank you, dear Paolo.'

'You did it yourself, Amy with your courage and determination.'

They watched the sun slowly sink over the water; the birds were hushed as if honouring this daily spectacle.

'Ah here you are!' It was Davide.

He halted as if he guessed he might have interrupted something but Paolo was already moving towards the restaurant, leaving them alone. They stood, his arm about her, watching the sky grow ashen as night came. A sudden terror of what dangers the darkness might hold engulfed her. She shivered.

Davide seemed to sense the chill was more than physical. 'Darling you're cold, let's go inside.'

Behind them the wedding party awaited, friends and family full of love and goodwill, to embrace them, to dispel present fears and whatever their unknown future unveiled. They turned towards the welcoming light.

FINE

Jennifer Pulling

Remember My Name is a work of fiction. Names, characters, events and incidents are the product of the author's imagination or used fictitiously. Any resemblance to actual persons, alive or dead, is purely coincidental.

ACKNOWLEDGEMENTS

My heartfelt thanks go to:

Alessandra Smith who gently guides me through the maze of Italian grammar.

Joan Fraser, my Shetland friend I've yet to meet, for her wise appraisal of my manuscript.

Beverley Elphick, treasured beta reader and writing buddy.

The dedicated volunteers of Torre Argentina cat sanctuary.

Andrew Kidd, who has navigated us many times through the streets of Rome.

Sheba, my beloved black cat, who has taught me much about feline habits and remains my constant writing companion.

Cover image by Gabriella Clare Marino. Instagram: @gabriella.clare and @gabriellaritratti

Cover design by Tony Gummer.

Last but not least, Rome, eternally my favourite city.

ABOUT JENNIFER PULLING

Jennifer Pulling is an author, playwright and journalist who has worked for many national newspapers and magazines. Her travel articles have been published widely in the UK and abroad. Her plays include *End of Story*, which examines the relationship of Harold and Primrose Shipman, and *The Swallow*, exploring the clash between Italian and English cultures. Previous books include *Feasting and Fasting*, *The Caring Trap*, *Monet's Angels*, *Monet's Shadow* and *If You Loved Me: A Story of Love, Loss And a Cat Called Leonardo,* the prequel to *Remember My Name*. *The Great Sicilian Cat Rescue* tells the story of her work with the feral cats of Sicily. To find out more about Jennifer please visit **www.jenniferpulling.co.uk**

Printed in Great Britain
by Amazon

21121193R00169